AMERICAN INVENTIONS AND INVENTORS

AMERICAN INVENTIONS AND INVENTORS

WILLIAM AUGUSTUS MOWRY,
ARTHUR MAY MOWRY

ISBN: 978-93-89679-60-1

Published: -

LECTOR HOUSE LLP
E-MAIL: lectorpublishing@gmail.com

WESTERN WHEAT FIELD
GIANT HARVESTER
MODERN SEWING MACHINE
WEAVING ON CHAIN LOOM
COLONIAL FIRE PLACE
PRINTING PRESS
TELEGRAPH
A CITY AT NIGHT
MODERN TRAVEL THE AUTOMOBILE

AMERICAN INVENTIONS AND INVENTORS

BY

WILLIAM A. MOWRY, A.M., PH.D.
AND ARTHUR MAY MOWRY, A.M.

Authors of "First Steps in the History of our Country," and "A History of the United States, for Schools."

PREFACE.

A school history should set forth such facts, and in such an order, as to show the progress of civilization. The great lessons of history are found in that line of events in the past which exhibits the progress of mankind — the uplift of humanity. The record of no other country can present a more startling array of forward movements and upward tendencies than that of our own land, and in no one direction does this upward movement appear quite so clearly as in the line of inventions.

Man's efforts are, first, to overcome nature. Food, shelter, and clothing are his primary wants. After these are supplied, he rises to higher realms of thought and action. Then he nourishes his intellect, exercises his sensibilities, and provides nutriment for his soul, that it, also, may grow. In this book the above logical order is followed.

It is painfully evident that many schoolchildren dislike the study of history. The authors of this book believe that this need not be. It is clear that the study should be undertaken at an earlier age than is usually the case in our public schools. It is not necessary, and oftentimes not desirable, that the books of history should be studied as text-books. Frequently they should be used as reading books. Such use is more likely to develop in the minds of the younger children a love for history.

This book, while adapted to older persons, has been prepared with special reference to the needs and capacities of children from ten to twelve years of age. It is commended to teachers and parents with full confidence that they will find it useful, and that the children will be both interested and profited by its perusal.

CONTENTS

SECTION III.
FOOD.

SECTION IV.
CLOTHING.

SECTION V.
TRAVEL.

CONTENTS

SECTION VI.
LETTERS.

LIST OF ILLUSTRATIONS

COUNT RUMFORD.

A NEW ENGLAND KITCHEN ONE HUNDRED YEARS AGO.

SECTION I.
HEAT

AMERICAN INVENTIONS AND INVENTORS.

CHAPTER I.

FIRE.

A TRAIN LEAVING THE STATION

"ALL aboard!" cries the conductor, and slowly the long train draws out of the San Francisco station on its way to Chicago and the Atlantic coast. Three sleepers, two chair coaches, passenger, baggage, and mail cars, loaded with travelers, trunks, and pouches of letters and papers; we are familiar with the sight of these heavy cars and the puffing engine which draws them. But what makes the train move? What power is great enough to do this? It is the power of steam, and steam is made from water by means of fire.

Now the long journey across the continent is over, and we are standing on the dock in New York City. Here we see the steamboat *Puritan*, thronged with passengers, ready to steam away from the wharf on its regular night trip to Fall River. For hours, perhaps, we have been watching the longshoremen as they have rushed back and forth, loading the great vessel with freight for New England. A few minutes later, as we see the majestic steamer, hundreds of feet long—larger than most city business buildings—slowly, but gracefully moving away from the dock, we say to ourselves, "Can it be that steam, caused by fire, has power enough to make the steamboat move through the water like this?"

While we watch the steamer glide around Castle Garden into East River, evening begins to come on; we must hasten uptown. As we pass along Broadway, lights flash out in the darkness and our thoughts are again turned to fire and steam. We have heard that the source of the electric light is in the dynamo, and that steam power is used to turn that great machine. The enormous engine, the mammoth boat, the brilliant light—all need the power of steam, and nothing but fire will produce this steam. What, then, is fire? and is its only use that of changing quiet, liquid water into powerful steam? Let us see.

Did you notice that machine shop which we passed when we were in Cleveland a few days ago? Did you see those furnaces with the huge volumes of flame bursting out of the open doors? You know that great heat is necessary to make tools and other implements of iron, and all the instruments of everyday life that are formed out of metals. Our pens and needles, our hoes and rakes, our horseshoes, our stoves and furnaces, our registers and the iron of our desks—all depend upon heat for their production. Fire can do much for us. To change water into steam is but one of its powers. Fire and heat are behind most of the operations of modern life.

As we open the door of the house we are met by a current of warm air rushing out into the chilly evening. It is the last of October, and in the middle of the day windows and doors have been left wide open to let in all the light and warmth of the bright sunshine. But it is evening now, and the sun has long since sunk below the horizon; it no longer gives us any of its heat. All night the air will grow colder and colder, and were we unprotected by clothing we should suffer from the chill atmosphere. Even coverings are not sufficient to keep the heat of our bodies from passing off into the air, just as the warm air rushed out through the open hall door. It has been found necessary to warm the air in our houses so that the bodily heat, which we need to sustain life, may not so easily be lost. The heat which the sun furnishes us is called natural heat; that which is produced by the skill of man is called artificial heat.

This artificial heat is used for a fourth purpose also. As we have seen, it makes steam for the locomotive, the steamboat, and other engines; it is necessary in the manufacture of tools and various utensils out of iron and other metals; and it warms our houses and schools, our offices and stores. It is also used everywhere and by everybody in cooking. Had we no fires or artificial heat of some sort we should have to eat our meat and fish raw; we could only mix our meal and flour with cold water, which would not be palatable to most of us; our vegetables, uncooked, would fail to satisfy us; and many of us would find ourselves limited to fruits and nuts, which would be hardly sufficient to keep us in good health, to say the least.

Have you ever thought that men or human beings are very much like other animals? Have you ever tried to find out the important differences between man and what are called the lower animals? One of these differences comes right in the line of our present thought. Dogs are fond of meat, and so are most people; but dogs do not need to have their meat cooked as we do. Horses whinny for their oats at night and morning; but they would not care for our favorite breakfast dish of cooked oatmeal. Bears are partly protected from the cold by their thick, shaggy coverings of fur; but even in very cold regions they have no warm fire around which to gather. Man is the "only fire-making animal," and to this fact he owes much of his power.

A VESTAL VIRGIN.

If we read the history of the world, and especially the story of the earlier life of the different nations and peoples, we shall find that fire was considered by them all to be one of the greatest blessings belonging to man. They thought that the gods whom they worshipped also treasured fire. The Romans offered sacrifices to Vesta, the goddess of the fireplace, and it was the duty of the vestal virgins to keep a fire always burning on her altar. Among the Greeks the hearth or fireplace itself was an object of worship.

These early peoples regarded the blessing of fire as so great that they believed it must have originally belonged to the gods alone. Many of them had traditions that the gods did not permit men in the earliest ages to have any knowledge or use of fire. Myths or stories have been found among the people of Australia, Asia, Europe, and America, telling how fire had been stolen from the gods and brought down to men. The best of these stories is that of the Greek, Prometheus, whose name means "forethought." This ancient mythical hero was supposed to have been the great friend and benefactor of mankind. But of all his gifts to men the most valuable was the gift of fire. According to the old myth, Prometheus went up into Olympus, the Greek heaven, and was welcomed by the gods. While there he examined the fire of the gods and thought what a blessing it would be to mankind. Acting under the advice of Athene, the goddess of wisdom, he stole some fire from the sun god, concealed it in a hollow reed, and brought it back with him to earth.

In early times there were no matches, and if a fire went out it was not easy to kindle it again. Probably the people wondered how the fire was made for the first time. They knew that it must have been obtained somehow, from somewhere; and out of this grew the story of Prometheus among the Greeks, and of the other fire stealers, the heroes of other peoples in all parts of the globe.

But all these stories of the fire of the gods and the way in which human beings were able to get hold of this priceless blessing we now know to be only myths. Students of early history are agreed that all men, everywhere, and at all times, have had the knowledge and the use of fire. Great differences exist between civilized and uncivilized people; the savages of interior Africa seem almost to belong to a different species of being from the cultured people of Europe and America; but all are able to warm themselves and to cook their food by means of burning fuel.

Civilized man has better arrangements for kindling his fire, better means of obtaining more good from it, and better ways for avoiding the smoke and other unpleasant features than has uncivilized man. A savage would not understand the modern chimney nor a kitchen range. He would be utterly at a loss to comprehend our modes of heating by the hot-air furnace or the coils of steam pipes. The forest provides him with all the wood that he needs for his fire, and he has little or no knowledge of coal or oil or gas.

Thus you and I are far in advance of the poor, half clad, half warmed savage; we are also in far more comfortable circumstances than were our ancestors who came from Europe to America two or three hundred years ago. In all the ages of the past until within a few hundred years little advance had been made in the methods of obtaining artificial heat. But since Columbus set sail from Spain, since John Cabot first saw the shores of this continent, since John Smith made friends with the Indians in Virginia, and William Bradford guided the lives of the Pilgrims at Plymouth, discoveries and inventions have changed most of our habits and customs as well as our surroundings. The methods of heating our houses and cooking our food have altered greatly, and we cannot fail to be interested in comparing the simple wood fires of long ago with the complex ways in which heat is now evenly distributed wherever it is wanted. For a little while, then, let us turn our thoughts to the primitive forms of heating and cooking which were common three centuries ago, and see in what ways the modern systems of providing artificial heat have been developed.

CHAPTER II.

INDIAN HOMES.

"Our homes and their surroundings are so familiar to us that it is hard for us to realize that our country was not always as it is now. Let us think about it. Have you seen any changes near where you live since you can remember? Have any new houses been built? Do you know of any old buildings that have been torn down in order that larger or better ones might take their places? Have you watched men making a new street or road, or, perhaps, working upon an old road to make it better? If you have, then you can think back to a time when some house that you can see to-day was not there; a time when there were not so many roads nor such good streets as now. Can you think back still further to a time when the house in which you live had not been built? when the street in front of your house had not been made? Can you imagine a time, still further back, when none of the houses in your city or village were standing? when there were no streets at all within sight of the place where you live? Then it will not be so very hard to think of the time, four hundred years ago, when there were no houses of wood, brick, or stone, such as we now see, anywhere in this country; when there was not a carriage road nor a street of any kind in the whole United States. We will try to imagine how this country looked before any white people lived in it, and before the cities and towns and villages and farms and ranches, that are so familiar to us, had been begun.

Four hundred years ago John Cabot sailed across the Atlantic Ocean and saw this country for the first time. As his little vessel moved along the coast, he looked upon bays and mouths of rivers which were very much as they are to-day. The peninsulas, the capes, and the islands were in the same places that they now are. They were, however, almost entirely covered with woods. Here and there were fields of grass, through which blue streams were flowing; but the larger part of what is now New England and the other Atlantic States was covered with thick forests. The trees were large and close together; their branches had never been cut off, and grew close to the ground. Shrubs and bushes filled all the space that was left between the larger trees, and made it almost impossible for any one to pass through. Wild animals had made paths for themselves, but if people had attempted to use these paths they would have been obliged to get down on their hands and knees and crawl through them. The rivers and the smaller streams of water were the best roads in those days; for unless they were shallow or flowed too swiftly down the rapids, boats could quite easily be pushed up stream as well as be carried down by the current.

In this country, covered with forests, were there only wild animals? Were there no human beings: no men, nor women, nor children? No white men lived in New England; the city of New York had not even been thought of; Baltimore and Savannah were impassable forests; and the great West was only a hunting ground. But the red men or American Indians did live in this country and were its only owners.

The Indians did not live in many roomed houses of wood or brick or stone; they never built roads or streets; nor did they ride in carriages. If they wished to go from one place to another they used canoes on the rivers as far as they could; if they wished to cross the land from one stream to another they made a foot path, called a trail. Sometimes a trail was broad enough to permit a canoe to be carried. Thus the Indians could travel long distances without growing tired from much walking.

The Indians must have had dwelling places to protect them from the cold and the storms which were as common then as now. Many tribes of Indians were in the habit of moving frequently from place to place, and for this reason their homes were not built for permanent use, but were made of materials that could be quickly put together. The Indians that lived in Canada and New England were more roving than those of New York; therefore their houses were very simple. They were long and narrow, with rounded roofs, and covered on the tops and sides with matting that could be readily removed.

The Iroquois, dwelling south of Lake Ontario, were a little more civilized than their neighbors, and built more permanent houses. Their dwellings were very long, from one to two hundred feet in length, and usually about thirty feet wide. The frames were made of long sticks or poles, set firmly in the ground; other poles formed the roof, with two sloping sides, over which were laid large strips of elm bark. These houses had a door at each end, with no windows, and light entered only through the doors and the large openings in the roof. The openings were made at frequent intervals to allow the escape of the smoke from the fires directly beneath.

Although the Indian dwellings varied greatly among the different tribes, in none of them did a family live by itself Usually twenty or more families dwelt together in each of the Iroquois "long houses." A building planned for twenty families had ten stalls or open closets as they might be called, arranged along each side. An open passageway ran the entire length of the house from door to door, in which were built five fires at equal distances. Each fire belonged to the four families whose stalls—two on each side—opened directly toward it.

Now let us imagine ourselves in one of these long houses, and let us try to see just how everything looked. Let us suppose that it is a little after sunset on a cold, stormy winter evening. We are glad to get under any covering in order to be somewhat protected from the biting wind and the stinging sleet. We have been welcomed by the Indians, have been made the guests of one of the families, and have been given something to eat. Supper over, we are able to look about us and to think whether we should consider ourselves cosy and comfortable if this were our own home.

The first thing that we observe is the fire, as it snaps and hisses. How warm it is, and how good it feels as we toast our cold hands and feet before it! But some-how we begin to wish that we were back beside our own stove. Then our eyes would not ache from the smoke. Why does it not go out at the top? It tries to, but the wind blows it back into the house so that, at times, it fills every corner, blinding our eyes, stifling our breath, and covering us with cinders from head to foot.

IROQUOIS LONG HOUSE

But as we sit, Turk fashion, squatted before the fire, we notice that we are being slowly covered up by something else than cinders. Although all the smoke does not go out at the opening, it seems as if almost all the snow did come in. At times it falls gently, slowly sifting into every fold in our clothing, into our eyes and ears, and gradually covering everything with its mantle of white. At other times a strong gust of wind sweeps down into the room, almost putting out the fire, and chilling us through and through in spite of the roaring blaze.

Now cold shivers begin to run down our backs. Besides, our limbs are grow-ing tired from sitting so long in the unusual position. So we think that we will try a change, and we decide to lie down at full length with our faces to the fire. It is not easy to move into the new position, because our neighbors are crowded so close to us; but we finally succeed. In a very few minutes our feet begin to ache with the cold and our faces seem burning up with the heat. Shall we change again, and for a time let our heads get cool while we warm our feet? We cannot keep this up all night, but we would need to do so if we tried to be really comfortable.

In this way the Indians lived. They had no beds, no separate chambers, no kitchen, dining room, nor parlor. In this one room, if it can be called a room, all the families ate and slept. Around these fires they spent their time while in the house. Here they lay stretched out for sleep, with skins of animals under them as a slight protection from the damp ground. They did not spend much time in changing their clothes, for they practically wore the same night and day. They really needed only the roof to cover them and the fire to warm them. Though the fire warmed them unevenly, though the smoke was uncomfortable, though the cold, the snow, and the rain came in at the opening and all around the sides of the house, yet the Indians had a covering, they had a fire, and they were to a great degree contented and happy.

INDIAN METHOD OF BROILING.

They were used to this life; they knew no other. Even after the white men came and the Indians had seen them in their houses, they had no desire to change their mode of living. "Ugh!" grunted an old redskin, as he studied the white man's ways;—"ugh! Injun make a little fire and set close to him; white man make a big fire and set way off."

The Indians needed food as well as covering. Their cooking must have been quite different from that which is done on a large modern kitchen range. They had no domestic animals except the dog; no cows nor pigs, no hens nor turkeys. They were compelled to hunt wild animals if they wanted meat. This meat they usually broiled; not on a broiler or a toaster, but upon slats or strips of wood placed above the fire. Fish was cooked in the same way. Sometimes they boiled the meat. For this they usually had wooden dishes, which could not be put over the fire. These were filled with water, into which red hot stones were placed. When the water had been heated the food was put in it to be cooked.

We should now have some idea of the manner of life among the Indians. We have learned a little about their houses and their habits; we have seen how they made their fires and did their cooking; we have heard about their trails and their canoes, and the way in which they traveled from place to place. Thus lived the American Indians or red men three or four hundred years ago, and thus they would probably be living to-day if Columbus or some one else had not discovered America; if the English, the French, and the Spaniards had not come across the ocean; if farms and villages, towns and cities had not sprung up all over the country; if the white men had not taken much of the land over which the Indians had roamed for centuries; and if the Indians had not learned much from the white men which has greatly changed their conditions.

CHAPTER III.

COLONIAL HOMES.

THE Indians, seated in their long community houses around their wood fires, ranging over their hunting ground seeking fresh meat, or stealthily creeping through the forest hoping to surprise some human enemy, at last found that they could no longer have this entire continent to themselves. More than four hundred years ago Europeans discovered the "New World" and began to explore it. More than three hundred years ago the Spaniards conquered the Indians in Mexico and made a settlement in Florida. Nearly three hundred years ago the French began to build homes in Canada, the Dutch in New York, and the English in Virginia and New England.

These white men, with their wives and children, crossed the Atlantic Ocean in the small vessels of those days, and built villages and cleared the land for farms. Their settlements were generally near the seacoast or the great rivers. The pioneers were thus nearer one another, and could the more readily hasten to each other's assistance in case of need.

The newcomers were not alike in appearance or habits. The French had different customs from the Spaniards. They not only spoke a different language, but they wore different kinds of clothes, tilled the soil in a different way, and lived in houses of different styles. The Dutch were quite unlike the English. Then, again, the life of the English in Virginia was different from life in New England: in the former colony some of the settlers were wealthy, owned large plantations, and lived at long distances from one another; in the latter the colonists had more nearly equal possessions, occupied smaller farms, and lived close together.

Although the colonists thus had differing habits and customs, in many respects they were much alike. They had come to a country where everything was new. No mills nor factories were run by the streams; no shops made clothing or farming tools; no stores sold furniture or groceries. Everything that the colonists needed must be either brought across the ocean or roughly made by themselves. Of course only the rich could afford the expense of bringing heavy articles three thousand miles in sailing vessels; therefore a large part of what the colonists wore or ate or used for furniture or buildings was rude and of home manufacture. A description of the mode of life in one section of the country will give something of an idea of how the colonists lived in other sections.

Almost the first thing that was necessary for the colonist to do, as soon as he had determined where he was to live, was to build his house; he began at once to fell the trees. The axe was one of the most important of his possessions and he soon learned to use it with great skill. If he needed his house immediately he usually built it of rough, unsplit logs, filling the spaces with clay and covering the roof with thatch.

PLYING THE AXE.

There is a story told of a log house which was built in the early part of one winter. The trees were cut when their trunks were frozen, and were laid in proper position to form the sides of the cabin. The stone chimney was built, and the house was ready. Day after day the great fireplace sent out its heat into the single room, until the sap in the logs was melted and little shoots with tender leaves began to form, which in time, at the ends of the logs nearest the fire, grew into long twigs. The logs had remained frozen on the outside, but had thawed within—a pleasant suggestion of the cheer and comfort found in a well warmed house.

If the newcomer had neighbors who could shelter his family for a time, he would split the logs and make a house somewhat tighter and better protected from cold and storm. After a time lumber mills were built and the logs were sawed into planks and boards. Many of the earliest New England houses contained but one room with an attic. The house was entered directly from out-of-doors, and was lighted by windows set with very small panes of glass or oiled paper. In one corner was the staircase, which sometimes was merely a ladder or perhaps a few cleats nailed on the framework. The furniture was meagre and most of it rudely made.

Can we see any improvement in this rough cottage over the Indian long house? It was more permanent; it was tighter and warmer; it was the abode of one family; it was a real home. In another respect the comfort of the log cabin was greatly increased: it had an enclosed fireplace and a chimney.

Some years ago fireplaces were seldom seen in our dwellings. In many of the old houses, in which the fireplaces were as old as the houses themselves, they were never used and were either boarded up or carefully screened from view. But more recently they have come into use again, and now seldom is a well arranged house built without one or more open fireplaces. We are then—most of us—acquainted with this small opening in the side or the corner of the room, in which small logs of wood burn upon the andirons or a bed of coals upon the grate. However, this modern grate or hearth is very unlike the huge fireplace of one and two centuries ago.

In the houses in which your great-grandmother and her mother and grandmother and great-grandmother lived the fireplace was not confined to a corner of the room, nor did it burn sticks fifteen or eighteen inches long. In the oldest house now standing in Rhode Island the fireplace was nearly ten feet long and about four feet in depth. Its back and sides were of stone, nearly two feet thick, and the chimney, thirteen feet by six, did not begin to narrow, as it went upward, until it reached the roof. This fireplace made an excellent play-house when the fire was out, and children found great delight in watching the stars from their seat in the chimney corner.

A COLONIAL FIREPLACE.

At first this open fireplace, with the fire burning in the centre, was the only means for cooking which our ancestors possessed. When they were able to build larger houses, with two, four, or eight rooms, even two stories high, they still had the great hearths; not one alone, but one in each of the principal rooms, and sometimes in the chambers. As time went on, stone or brick ovens were built by the side of the fireplaces, and frequently tin or "Dutch" ovens were brought across the ocean and used in case of need. Let us look into one of these old houses on a

Saturday, or "baking day," and notice some of the pleasures and inconveniences of cooking in olden time.

When Mother Brown rises at half past four in the morning she dresses quickly, for the coals, which had been carefully covered up, have given out little heat during the bitter, cold night. Before she can wash her hands and face she must start up the fire, for all the water in the house is frozen. She carefully rakes off the ashes from the coals which are still "alive," deftly lays on them a few shavings and pieces of bark, and, when they begin to burn brightly, piles upon them small and then larger sticks of wood. Now Father Brown and John, the hired man, who have come in from doing the chores, lift on to the fire one of the six foot logs, three or four feet in circumference, which have been previously brought in. Then Mother Brown calls the children. Ruth, the eldest, is already nearly dressed; Mehitable, just in her teens, is soon ready; while Polly, "the baby," nearly eight years old, finds it hard work to crawl out from between the sheets. The boys are even harder to rouse, for mother has to call Nathaniel, aged eleven, three times before he appears, and Joseph, two years younger, is slower still.

We will not stop to notice the breakfast, which is eaten, and the dishes washed, long before the sun rises. Now the outside door opens and in comes the old white horse, hauling a great backlog. John unhitches the chain and rolls the log upon the fire. This done, the horse goes out at the door opposite the one he entered. Father Brown brings in several armfuls of brush and heavier sticks, and throws them down near the fireplace.

As this is baking day, the oven must be made ready The great brick oven, one side of which makes also one side of the fireplace, is filled with the brush and light wood, which is soon burning briskly. For an hour the fire is kept up, new wood being thrown in when necessary; then it is allowed to go out. Meanwhile Mother Brown and Ruth are busy—mixing and rolling, sifting rye and Indian meal, stirring up eggs, and adding milk and butter. By the time the oven is heated the cooks are ready to use it; and Mehitable rakes out the coals and ashes with a long stick, shaped like a shepherd's crook.

First the pans of "rye 'n' Injun" bread are laid in the oven, away back at the farther end. Then the "pandowdy" or great apple pudding and the "Injun" pudding are placed in front of the bread. While the bread and the puddings are baking, two tin ovens are brought in and prepared for use. These Dutch ovens are mere sheets of metal curved around into more than half a circle, with the opening placed toward the fire. A long iron rod runs through from side to side of the oven on which the meat for roast is to be spitted. Mother Brown removes one of the spits and thrusts it through a piece of beef, and in the same way spits a fat turkey on the other. Here is work for little Polly, upon whom rests the task of frequently turning the spit so that the meat is evenly roasted.

Later in the day, when the bread is baked, the oven is heated again and filled with pies—apple, mince, squash, and pumpkin. By the time these are baked the day is done. The coals on the hearth are covered with ashes and the tired cooks gladly retire for the night.

HAULING IN A BACKLOG.

COOKING IN A COLONIAL KITCHEN.

On other days meat is boiled in pots that are hung from the crane, a long, swinging, iron rod which reaches directly over the fire or may be turned out into the room. Upon the hearth potatoes are baked, corn is roasted, and other primitive forms of cooking are used. We have made a long step from the Indian's open fire and his simple cooking to the brick and tin ovens and the metal pots and kettles of our ancestors; but is it not a longer step to the coal, oil, and gas ranges of to-day?

CHAPTER IV.

CHIMNEYS.

REMEMBERING our experience in the Indian long house—the discomfort of the smoke and the opening in the roof—we shall understand another great improvement in the colonist's house. Even the log cabin had its chimney. The rising column of hot air from the fire, carrying the smoke with it, is confined between walls of stone or brick, and the room is fairly free from smoke. Why did not the Indian build a chimney? The temporary nature of his dwelling may have been a partial reason; but the red man's lack of civilization was doubtless the most effective cause. Even many so-called civilized nations built their houses without chimneys, and in fact this convenience is but a few centuries old.

The ancient Greeks are praised for their high civilization, and yet they were little better off than the savage Indians of the New World in the methods of heating their houses. Neither the Greeks nor the Romans had chimneys for their dwellings. It is true that Greece and Italy are warmer countries than England or most of the United States, and doors and windows could be left open with less discomfort than with us. Much of the smoke might thus escape, but enough doubtless remained to be unpleasant. The Greeks refrained from carving the rooms in which fires were built, for they realized that such ornamentation would soon be discolored by soot.

After Greece had been conquered by the Romans and Rome had been overthrown by the Germanic tribes, much of the ancient civilization was lost and the "Dark Ages" followed. During this period the people throughout Europe made their fires in holes in the centre of the room, under an opening in the roof—just as we have seen that the Indians did. When the family went to bed at night they covered the hole in the roof with a board and also threw ashes over the coals, to prevent the wooden house from catching fire while they slept. It was the custom in every town, for many centuries, to ring the curfew or "cover-fire" bell each night, warning the inhabitants to cover their fires, put out their lights, and go to bed.

The first chimneys were probably built in Northern Italy about seven hundred years ago. The story is told that the Lord of Padua went to Rome in 1368 and found no chimney in his hotel. The Romans still held to the custom of kindling their fires in openings in the ground in the middle of the room. The Lord of Padua, longing for the comforts to which he was accustomed, sent to Padua for carpenters and masons, and had them build two chimneys like those at home. On the top of these he had his coat of arms affixed.

Gradually chimneys came into use throughout Europe, and when the colonists came to America they built them as a matter of course. As we have seen, the fireplaces were mammoth, and the chimneys therefore were also of great size; and for this reason, although the discomfort from the smoke was less than in the Indian long houses, it was not wholly avoided. For centuries, however, people had been used to the smoke, which occasionally poured back into the room instead of going up the chimney, and it did not occur to them, any more than to the red men, that it could be avoided. Not until a New England boy, who was then living in England, began to study into the cause of smoking chimneys was any relief obtained.

Benjamin Thompson was born in Woburn, Massachusetts, and had just come to manhood when the American Revolution broke out. Partly owing to certain family connections, he took the side of King George III., and went to England. After the war was over he went to Bavaria, entered the service of the king, and became his chamberlain. He rose through various positions until he became minister of war, and was made Count Rumford. He remained in Bavaria a few years, then lived for a time in England, and spent his last days in Paris.

Both in Bavaria and in England, Count Rumford devoted himself to science and the improvement of the conditions of his fellow men. It would be interesting to know the steps that he took and the good that he did, but we can here notice only some of his improvements in the methods of heating houses. As a scientist he was asked to "cure" smoking chimneys, and he succeeded so well that he once said he had "cured" more than five hundred in London alone.

He found out the simple fact that smoke will readily go up a chimney, unless there is something to stop it. All that was necessary was to discover the trouble and remove it. In nearly all of the five hundred chimneys nothing more was needed than to make the lower part of the chimney and the fireplace of the right form and size. One firm of builders was kept constantly employed carrying out his suggestions. Not only did he "cure" the chimneys, but he also prevented the waste of much heat. In accordance with his directions the square fireplace was changed so that the sides made a greater angle with the back and would therefore reflect more heat into the room. He also made the space about the fire smaller, thus rendering the air hotter and therefore more ready to rush up the chimney, carrying more of the smoke with it. Count Rumford's ideas have been generally followed since his day, and now fireplaces seldom give out smoke into the room while they furnish more heat.

Count Rumford next took up the problem of improving stoves. Before we consider his improvements, however, we must note something about the first stoves. Another Massachusetts boy, born nearly half a century before Benjamin Thompson, also became a scientist, inventor, and discoverer. Benjamin Franklin was a traveler and in many other respects was like Count Rumford. But he chose to go with the colonies when they revolted from Great Britain, and he gave all his services to his fellow countrymen. A few years before the birth of Thompson, Franklin made an invention which was the first improved method of heating rooms. There had been so-called German stoves before his day, but they were not much used in this country.

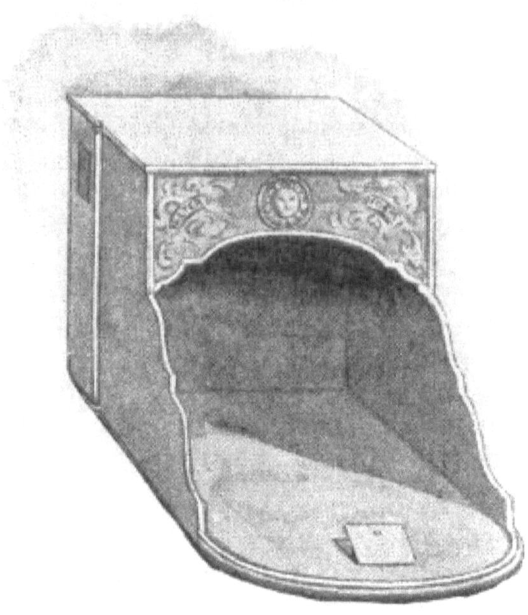

A FRANKLIN STOVE.

It was in 1742 that Franklin, while in Philadelphia, devised the "Franklin stove" or "Pennsylvania fireplace." It consisted of iron sides, back and top, and was entirely open in front. A flue was arranged in the back which connected with the chimney to carry off the smoke. This movable fireplace was designed to burn wood, comparatively small logs being used. It had many advantages over the stone fireplace. It was set up nearer the middle of the room, thus sending heat out in all directions and warming the entire room. It saved much of the heat which had previously passed directly up the chimney and been lost. In the Pennsylvania fireplace this heat warmed the iron on the top of the stove and at the back, as well as the flue itself, all of which warmed the air in the room. Saving the heat saved wood also. Franklin himself said:

"My common room, I know, is made twice as warm as it used to be, with a quarter of the wood I formerly consumed there."

Franklin was offered a patent for his device by the governor of Pennsylvania, but he declined it. He declared that inasmuch as "we enjoy great advantages from the inventions of others, we should be glad of an opportunity to serve others by any invention of ours." Unfortunately, however, the people did not obtain from his generosity all the advantages that Franklin expected, for a London iron manufacturer made some slight changes in the pattern, not improving the stove in the least, and obtained a patent. From the sale of these stoves he made what was called "a small fortune."

Franklin's fireplace was but the first in a long series of inventions that have brought to us the stove of to-day. The great merit in his work was the idea of giving up the stone fireplace for one of iron. Changes in the form and shape of the stove have followed as a matter of course. No special credit is due to any one else, unless it be to Count Rumford, who, after curing the chimneys, made a cook stove with an oven. Then, for the first time since men knew how to cook over a fire, cooking could be carried on and the cook be protected from the direct heat of the fire.

Thus we come to the modern house with its modern stoves. No longer have we but one method of heating a dwelling. Sometimes a stove is set up in each of the rooms. Sometimes a larger stove is placed in the cellar, and this furnace heats air that is carried by large pipes or flues to the rooms, where the heated air comes out through registers. Sometimes a furnace in the cellar heats water, and hot water or steam is sent through small pipes, and passing through coils or radiators gives out heat. Besides, the cooking range is found in most kitchens.

All these systems of heating houses exist instead of the old-fashioned fireplace. Even when the modern grate is built, it is usual to find a register or steam coil on the opposite side of the room, because the open fire is apt to warm one side of the room only. It is pleasant, however, to look into a blazing fire, and we are sometimes almost willing to have the heat unevenly distributed if only we can watch the flames.

Some form of the stove, however, is our main dependence, and its various developments have been due, generally, to the desire of being freed from the discomforts of the old time methods. Perhaps also the growing scarcity of wood and the discovery of coal have had some effect upon the development of the stove; but that we must leave to another chapter.

CHAPTER V.

FUEL.

"WHAT do you burn in the stoves in your houses?" was asked of a class of schoolchildren in a small Pennsylvania town. Hands went up in every direction; one said "kerosene oil"; two others shouted "gas"; a few replied "wood"; most of the class answered "coal." Then the teacher made further inquiries to learn why these different substances were used. The three who answered gas and oil agreed that coal was burned in other stoves in their houses, but that oil and gas stoves were used also because they were so convenient.

When the question was asked why coal was used, instantly the answer was given that coal was the best thing to burn; everybody burned it. Now this was not quite true, but Miss Turner, the teacher, instead of immediately correcting the error, turned to the pupils who had answered "wood," and inquired why they used wood. One said, "We haven't any coal"; another thought that it was because wood kindled more easily than coal; a third was sure that he was right—"We don't have to buy wood; coal costs money."

Now this boy had the correct idea. He lived in the country, though near the town. His father owned a large farm, a part of which was still forest land; he could cut his own wood, and therefore did not buy coal. After a few more questions the teacher discovered that all those who burned wood lived some little distance from town.

Then she turned to the class again and asked them if they could now tell why the town families used coal instead of wood. One said, "We do not own forests." Another thought that it was because there were not trees enough. A third shook his hand wildly and shouted, "Coal is cheaper than wood!" A shy little girl ventured to suggest, "Because coal is better than wood; it lasts longer."

"You have each of you given a good reason," Miss Turner answered. "Coal is cheaper than wood here in the town because wood is growing more and more scarce. Many of your parents prefer coal because with it the fire needs less attention. But the coal dealers charge more to carry coal out into the country, and those who still own forests find it cheaper to burn their own wood. What sort of replies would I have received if I had asked the same questions of children in Pennsylvania Colony, or in any of the colonies, one hundred and fifty or two hundred years ago?"

The children had studied history somewhat. They knew the story of Columbus and his discoveries; they had read of the Pilgrims and the Puritans; they could have answered questions concerning John Smith and Henry Hudson; and they were especially familiar with William Penn and the Quakers, with George Washington and Braddock's defeat. But not one of them remembered that he had ever been told anything about the fires of the colonists.

There was a pause for a time; then one boy asked, "Didn't they burn just what we burn?" After another pause the shy little girl asked, "Didn't they have more forests then than now?" Before the teacher could reply, a boy said, "Perhaps they did not have any coal."

The children had thus thought it out for themselves, and they were right. Miss Turner then told them that it was many years after the time of Columbus or Hudson or Penn before coal mines were discovered in this country or coal used. She added that almost all the country, from Maine to Georgia and westward across the Alleghany Mountains, was covered with thick forests when the colonists crossed the Atlantic Ocean.

"What do you suppose our ancestors thought of these forests? Were they glad to see them, or did they wish that they covered less ground?" asked the teacher.

Most of the children answered that the forests must have been of great value to the colonists; they would not have to pay anything for fuel.

"Can you raise vegetables or grain in the woods?" was Miss Turner's next question.

Then the pupils began to see that the forests were hindrances as well as helps. The teacher told them that they gave the colonists more wood than was needed for fires and for lumber. She added that every acre of ground that they wished to plant with Indian corn or rye, with potatoes or squashes, must first be freed from the trees. Before the land could be plowed it must be cleared. If, then, the trees furnished more wood than could be used, it was natural for the farmer to burn the trees and stumps in the fields.

If there had been but few settlers and if they had been widely scattered over a large territory, no harm would have resulted. But the colonists came over by the thousands and had large families of children. By the time the country had been settled a hundred years, great gaps had been made in the forests. A few of the most foresighted of the colonists began to think about the future and to wonder what they would do for fuel if the wood should give out. In fact, trees began to be scarce in the neighborhood of the larger towns, and firewood as well as lumber became expensive.

"Suppose that all the forests in this country had been destroyed," the class was asked, "what would the people have done for fuel?"

"Used coal," replied a boy from a back seat.

"Yes," said Miss Turner, "if there were any coal, and if the colonists knew where to find it and how to use it. But what is this coal and where does it come from?"

"We owe all our knowledge of the origin of coal to the geologists, who have made a careful study of the surface of the earth," continued Miss Turner. "They tell us that there was a time when human beings did not live on the earth; when not even animals that need to breathe the air could exist. The atmosphere which surrounded the earth in those days was different from the air which we breathe. We need the oxygen that is in our air to sustain life; poor ventilation in our rooms or halls soon renders them uncomfortable and often causes our heads to ache. The reason for this is the presence in the air of too large a quantity of a gas called carbonic acid gas; an extra amount of it makes the air unfit to breathe, but a certain amount is necessary to sustain plant life.

"In the coal-forming or carboniferous age the atmosphere around the earth contained less oxygen than at present and great quantities of carbonic acid gas. For this reason, as I have said, animals did not exist, but plants—large shrubs, great ferns, and huge trees—lived and grew vigorously. If we have ever seen thick woods we need only imagine all the bushes and trees of the forest to be of enormous size in order to have some idea of the vegetable growth of the carboniferous age. The earth was preparing vast quantities of fuel to be ready, thousands of years later, for the millions of men that were to come.

"The growth of the forests was but one step in the preparation of coal. The second step was the submerging of the forests, covering them with water as if at the bottom of the sea. Then the streams brought gravel, sand, and mud into this ocean, and these were hardened into clay and sandstone by the pressure of the water, perhaps aided by the heat of the earth itself. The trees and ferns were bent down and pressed together and driven into the most compact condition possible.

"But again earthquakes came and the water disappeared. The layer of clay and sandstone was covered with soil which became dry enough to produce other forests, growing as rank as the first. These were again overwhelmed and covered first with water, then with rocks and soil, only to be lifted again for another growth. This process was repeated in some cases many times, as we can see with a little study."

Here Miss Turner stopped and said: "Next Saturday, if it is pleasant, we will have our annual spring picnic. We will go to a new place this time. We will try Howland's Grove, and then in the afternoon we will go down into the Jefferson mine and see what it is like."

We have not time to read about the picnic, nor of the interest that the class showed before the appointed Saturday, as well as all the forenoon of that day. Nor can we tell how the children went down the shaft of the mine, and how they were at first so quiet that hardly a word was said. The teacher showed them a layer of coal in the mine which was about three feet thick. Just above it was a rock which was different from the coal. This they were told was sandstone, the hardened sand which had been heaped upon the forests so many thousand years before. Then below the coal was another rock which was entirely unlike either the coal or the sandstone. This was the seat-stone, the rock made out of the soil in which the forest had grown. Then below this they found three more layers, sandstone, coal, and seat-stone, and so on until the bottom of the mine was reached.

By this time the children were ready to ask questions.

"Oh, Miss Turner, what is this curious-looking thing in this part of the seat-stone?" asked one of the boys.

Miss Turner replied: "That is a fossil. It is part of a root of a tree, and has retained its shape and appearance all these thousands and thousands of years."

IN A COAL MINE.

One of the miners who had been listening to the conversation said: "If you will step this way, madam, I can show you the whole of a tree-trunk in the coal."

The children eagerly crowded around as the miner showed the fossilized trunk of a tree still standing just as it grew, with its roots in the seat-stone and its top in the sandstone above the coal—for here the layer of coal was several feet in thickness.

A few minutes afterward, as the children were looking carefully at the sides of the mine to see if they could find more fossils, the shy little girl said quietly to the teacher: "I think that I have found something, Miss Turner; won't you please see?"

She led the way to a trunk which showed the various stages in the process of change. One end was still almost like wood, the middle part was a very soft brown coal, while the other end was true coal.

"That helps us to understand more about the way in which the forests were changed to coal," said Miss Turner. "Now here is one more proof that coal was formed out of wood."

The teacher picked up a piece of coal and broke it with a hammer. Then she showed on the new surface some patches of a black substance. "Does not that look like charcoal?" she asked. "You know that charcoal is wood partly burned."

Thus the class learned how nature, ages and ages ago, began to prepare for the use of man a fuel which seems inexhaustible, is superior to wood in many respects, and is freely distributed in various portions of the world. This coal, which has taken the place of wood to a great extent in furnishing heat for our houses and stores, is found in large quantities in the United States, but was not mined or used here until the middle of the last century.

CHAPTER VI.

COAL.

THE use of coal for heating purposes is so familiar to every one nowadays that probably few have ever thought about the time when it was unknown. Coal was as plentiful three thousand years ago as it is now. Layers and beds of the fuel existed just under the surface of the ground, and in many places cropped out through it. But the stones were merely "black rocks," and the idea that rocks would burn was too absurd to occur to any one. We may well wonder how it was first discovered that coal would burn.

Professor Greene suggests a possible explanation of this discovery. "There is in coal a hard, yellow, brassy mineral which flies in the fire and not infrequently startles the circle that has gathered around its cheerful blaze. When exposed to damp air this mineral undergoes chemical change, and during the process heat is given out, sometimes in sufficient quantities to set the coal alight. In this way it occasionally happens that seams of coal, when they lie near the surface, take fire of their own accord. One day a savage on a stroll was startled by finding the ground warm beneath his feet, and by seeing smoke and sulphurous vapors issuing from it. He laid it first to a supernatural cause; but curiosity getting the better of superstition, he scraped away the earth to find whence the reek came. Then he saw a bed of black stone, loose blocks of which he had already noticed lying about; parts of this stone were smouldering, and as soon as air was admitted burst into a blaze."

Whether coal was thus discovered or not, its first discovery must have occurred early in the history of the world. More than twenty centuries ago the Greek scholar, Theophrastus, wrote of the coals which were used by blacksmiths. There are indications that coal was mined in England before that country was conquered by the Romans. But not until the twelfth century was enough of the mineral mined in Newcastle, the great coal region of England, to warrant its being carried to London. As this coal was brought in vessels to the metropolis it received the name of "sea-coal," and it was thus called for several centuries.

How strange it is that opposition always arises to every new thing! People are always to be found who think that anything with which they are not familiar cannot be good. So it was in London. A cry began to arise that the use of coal was injurious to health. The coal was soft or bituminous, and burned with considerable flame and a dense smoke. This was before the common use of chimneys, and therefore the air in the rooms where it was burned became filled with an unpleasant odor. The belief was general that the use of coal rendered the air unfit to breathe, and Parliament was requested to put a stop to it. King Edward I. issued a proclamation forbidding any but blacksmiths to burn sea-coals, and directing that buildings from which coal-smoke was seen to come should be torn down. Though the law was repealed under a later king, coal was but little used for household purposes until the eighteenth century.

Most of the coal beds in the United States are situated at some distance from the ocean; therefore the first colonists, settling along the coast, were for a long time ignorant of their existence. The first white man to discover coal was Father Hennepin, who more than two hundred years ago, while exploring the Mississippi River, found it in Illinois. The first mines worked were the Richmond fields in Virginia, where coal was taken out a century and a half ago.

There is a tradition that a boy left home one morning to go fishing. After trying his luck for a time he found that his bait was gone. Accordingly he began to hunt for crawfish, and while searching stumbled over some black stones which attracted his attention. He had found the "outcrop" of a coal bed, and on his return he made known his discovery. A rich vein of coal was soon disclosed, and mining on a small scale was begun. We must remember that this story is only tradition and may not be true. We might wonder, perhaps, how the boy knew that the stones were any different from other rocks except in being black.

The way in which a twelve-foot vein was discovered in Pennsylvania is told in *Forest and Stream*, and is probably quite true.

Elias Blank, living in Western Pennsylvania in the latter part of the last century, was called to his door one night and found there Lewis Whetzell, a famous Indian fighter, and Jonathan Gates, commonly called "Long Arms."

"Friend Lewis," said Mr. Blank, "where have thee and our friend been, and where bound?"

"I want to get out of here at once," said Whetzell, "and Long Arms is of the same opinion. This country's bewitched, and Long Arms and I are nearly scared to death."

"Friend Lewis, thee must not tell such stories to me," said old Elias. "Thee knows I am thy friend, and I have saved thee when a price was on thy head. I know thou art a man of courage, and friend Jonathan Gates, whom some call 'Long Arms,' fears nothing on earth, and I'm fearful nothing anywhere else; and yet thou tellest me that he and thee are scared even almost to death. Shame on thee so to declare before thy friend, who loves ye both as he were thy father!"

"No, no, Elias," said Whetzell, dropping into the Quaker speech. "I tell thee no lie. We are scared. Yesterday afternoon we were in hiding about a mile from Dunkard Creek, and in the evening we built a fire under the bank very carefully; and we got some black rocks to prop up a little kettle, and put them beside the fire rather than in it; and the black rocks took fire and burned fiercely, with a filthy smoke and a bright light; and Long Arms said the devil would come if we stayed; and we grabbed the kettle and poured out the water, and made our way here, leaving the black rocks to burn."

Elias Blank was much interested. He did not tell Whetzell what the black rocks were, but he found out exactly where the men had made their fire, and the next day hunted up the camping-ground, found the "black rocks" in one of the river-hills, and opened a coal bank.

Thus, a little here and a little there, coal was discovered and used. At first it was mingled with wood, and then burned alone on the hearth. This coal was easily kindled, for it was bituminous or soft; it was not necessary to provide an extra draft, or to spend much more time in lighting it than had been customary with wood. Not many years passed, however, before a variety of coal was found that was hard and would not kindle easily. Accordingly it was thrown aside as useless. This was anthracite coal, and it is now generally preferred to the bituminous because of this very quality. Being hard, it does not burn away so rapidly; besides, it needs less attention and gives out much less smoke.

BLACKSMITH AT HIS FORGE.

Just before the Revolution, Obadiah Gore, a blacksmith in the Wyoming valley in Pennsylvania, tried hard coal in his forge. At first, even with his great bellows, he was unable to make it burn. He continued the experiment, however, and after a time the lumps began to yield and flames darted from them. He thus discovered that pieces of anthracite coal could be kindled and burned if there was a "strong current of air," as he said, "sent through them by the bellows; without that I could do nothing with them."

Mr. Gore thus used anthracite coal in his forge, but even he did not burn it at home. Not until the beginning of this century was hard coal used for domestic purposes. Oliver Evans in 1803 successfully burned it in a grate. Many years passed, however, before hard coal came into common use. A few people purchased anthracite coal, but they could not burn it; they used it just as they had been accustomed to use soft coal. After that, great difficulty was experienced in persuading any one to try the new coal.

Nicholas Allen in Pennsylvania discovered anthracite coal and got out several wagonloads of it. He tried in vain to sell it. "No," said the people, "we have tried that once, and we do not propose to be cheated again." Mr. Allen became discouraged and sold his interest to his partner, Colonel Shoemaker, who took the coal to Philadelphia. Here he praised it so highly that at last a few people bought a little for trial. They continually punched the coal and stirred up the fire, but they did not succeed in making it burn. They became enraged with Colonel Shoemaker, and procured a warrant for his arrest as a common impostor. The colonel heard of the warrant, quietly left the city, and drove thirty miles out of his route in order to avoid the officer. Fortunately a firm of iron factors who had purchased some of the coal succeeded in making it burn. They announced the fact in the Philadelphia newspapers, and other iron-workers tried the coal. Soon all the furnaces were using it.

Both anthracite and bituminous coal are freely mined in various sections of the United States. There is coal enough underground to last for many centuries. It used to be said that England was the great coal-mining country, for her coal fields are nearly as extensive as those of all the rest of Europe. But the United States has a supply of coal that will apparently be hardly diminished when that of the British Islands is entirely used. The single State of Pennsylvania has a greater store of coal than all Europe, and her part is less than one-tenth of the stock of coal in the United States.

Even if the forests of the entire country should be destroyed, we should not want for fuel. But let us remember that not only would the loss of our forests deprive us of wood for other purposes than merely to keep us warm, but it would also cause great injury to the farming interests of the country. If we would have good crops we must have proper rainfalls; without forests the rain would do greater and greater injury and less and less good. We ought to do all in our power to help preserve our forests, and as far as we can to increase the number of trees.

CHAPTER VII.

MATCHES.

"Thomas! Thomas! The fire is out! Get right up and go over to neighbor Wallace's and borrow some fire." It was a cold morning, eight degrees below zero, and Mr. Wallace lived three-quarters of a mile away. The sun would not rise for two hours; but, when mother called, the boys instantly obeyed. Thomas hurriedly dressed, snatched a shovel which was standing by the hearth, and hastily shutting the outside door, ran as fast as he could to the nearest neighbor's. Of course he hurried, for was not mother all dressed and not a bit of fire in the house? The fire must have died down too much the evening before; and although the coals had been carefully covered with ashes before father and mother went to bed, mother could not find a tiny spark anywhere under the ashes in the morning.

Thomas kept up his run until he was tired, and then fell into a brisk walk. When he reached neighbor Wallace's, he was glad to warm his numbed fingers over the raging fire in the fireplace. But he knew that he must not stop long, so he stated his errand, and Mrs. Wallace placed some live coals on his shovel and thoroughly covered them with ashes. Thomas rested a moment longer and then hastened home; for if those coals should be out when he reached the house he would have to make the trip over again.

This disaster did not befall him, however, and soon his mother had placed the coals on the hearth and had laid upon them a few shavings. These kindled at once; small sticks were soon ablaze, and in a very short time the fire was burning as vigorously as the neighbor's had been.

The boys of two centuries ago fully realized what it meant to have the fire go out. Perhaps the nearest neighbors were not always so far distant, but it was no pleasant task to be sent for coals any distance on a winter morning. If, however, no neighbors were near and coals could not be borrowed, how under circumstances like these could a new fire be kindled? If we wanted a fire nowadays we might say, "Strike a light," because we should obtain the light by striking a match; but, before matches were invented, the expression used would probably have been, "Rub a light."

An early method of producing a light, and from this a fire, was by rubbing two sticks together. If this process be continued long enough the wood will become heated and sparks will fly off. Then, in order to start the fire, it is only necessary to catch one of these sparks upon something that will burn easily. This method was used thousands of years ago, and is still common among the savages in various parts of the globe. This seems simple enough, but if you try it you will find that it is no easy task. It requires considerable muscular power to "rub a light" from two sticks of wood, and almost any other process is preferable.

THOMAS CARRYING FIRE.

The most important thing in this method of kindling a fire is the rapidity with which the sticks are rubbed together. Some one of the savages more keen than the others conceived the idea that he could save labor and at the same time increase the rapidity with which the stick moved. He took his bow and twisted the cord once around a stick. Then he placed one end on a piece of wood, and by moving the bow back and forth twisted the stick with great rapidity. Soon the shavings which he had placed at the point of contact were ablaze. Little by little this drill was improved, and now among some of the American Indians it furnishes a comparatively easy way of kindling a fire.

Most children have seen a spark caused by the shoe of a horse striking a stone in the road. Sometimes if one stone strikes another a spark is produced. All this was perceived even in the earliest times, and the best substances to be used became well known. The stone called flint was found to be the best for one of the two substances, and steel is usually preferred for the other. When steel and flint strike each other, if a spark falls upon some vegetable matter a fire is soon kindled.

Perhaps the most common substance used to catch the spark was touchwood, a soft, decayed wood carefully broken into small fragments. After a time, in place of the touchwood, tinder was used, which was made by scorching old linen handkerchiefs. Later the tinder box was invented, in which a steel wheel was spun like a top upon a piece of flint set in tinder. After the discovery of gunpowder, flint and steel were used in guns. A hammer of flint struck an anvil of steel, and the spark produced fell into a pan of gunpowder, causing the flash which fired the gun.

TINDER BOX, FLINT, AND MATCHES.

Before the American Revolution, and even into the present century, the process of kindling a fire was not a simple one. The most frequent means employed, as has been seen, was the borrowing of coals from a neighbor. Less often, recourse was had to the long and difficult process of rubbing a spark from two pieces of wood. Sometimes, among the well-to-do, the tinder box was used; but it was seldom satisfactory. For these reasons the fire was always most carefully watched; every precaution was taken to prevent it from going out. Seldom could the house be left by the whole family for any length of time, and all because of the lack of a match.

Matches are a result of the study of chemistry. During the Dark Ages a few scholars were interested in what they called alchemy; but they spent most of their time and thought in trying to discover two things—how to change iron into gold, and how to keep themselves eternally young. About two hundred years ago these two foolish desires came to be considered unpractical, and since then chemists have been constantly seeking to discover ways of benefiting mankind. For many years students in different countries tried to find certain chemicals that could be so combined as to render the tinder box unnecessary. Several of these attempts to make a light seemed successful, but most of them were dangerous and all were expensive. An account of one of these trials may be of interest.

About seventy years ago a young man named Lauria, in Lyons, France, watched his professor pound some sulphur and chlorate of potash together. The resulting flash and sharp crack set him thinking, and he went home and began to experiment. He had a few sticks of pine wood which had been partly dipped in sulphur, and a few glass tubes, and he obtained more sulphur and some chlorate. He tried melting and mixing, only to meet with many accidents. Finally he dipped the end of one of the sticks into sulphur and then into the chlorate. He observed that some of the chlorate remained on the stick. Then he rubbed this prepared end on the wall where there happened to be a little phosphorus; the stick immediately blazed. He had discovered for himself the principle of the match; all he needed besides was something which would make the chlorate always stick to the sulphured wood.

However, this match was not satisfactory and was never manufactured for sale. Phosphorus was dangerous, and it was not safe to have it spread upon a wall or any other surface. The first matches of practical use were made in 1833, and were invented by six different men in six different countries. These were the original Lucifer matches, which did not require the use of phosphorus. They were made of thin sticks of wood partly covered with sulphur. The ends of these sticks were then dipped into a compound of chlorate of potash, sulphite of antimony, and gum. When used these matches were drawn through a bent piece of sandpaper. They were costly, frequently selling for a cent apiece.

A few years later a famous chemist discovered the red form of phosphorus, which is not dangerous to handle. Since that time most matches have contained this substance in the mixture, although during the last half century hundreds of different combinations have been invented. To-day hardly any article is manufactured that is so common and inexpensive as the match. Without it we should feel almost lost, and surely it would seem to us that the Dark Ages had returned. We are told that the inhabitants of the United States use on an average more than a thousand matches a year each. There are more than forty manufactories in this country, most of them being in California, Connecticut, New York, and Pennsylvania, yet the entire business is principally controlled by one great company.

During the last two hundred years chimneys have been improved, stoves have been invented and developed, coal has been discovered, and matches have come into universal use. The log cabins of our ancestors have been replaced by the well-built houses of to-day. The mammoth fireplaces, sending much heat up the chimney and much smoke into the room, have given way to the stoves and furnaces that render life comfortable. No longer is it necessary to freeze our backs while roasting our faces. Cranes, pot-hooks and trammels, and Dutch ovens are chiefly to be seen in museums, and the kitchen range saves the cook much needless labor. Nowadays we seldom find the fires out on a winter's morning and the water frozen in the pitcher. Instead of hastening through the cold and the snow to a neighbor to borrow fire, we simply "strike a match." We all of us live in comfort that would have seemed luxury to the wealthiest families two centuries ago.

Can we look forward to the changes that may come in the future in the methods of heating our houses and cooking our food? Already railroad cars are being heated by steam from the engines and electric cars are heated by electricity. Already oil stoves and gas stoves have come into common use and are found to possess many advantages: No ashes need removal; the fire may be started without delay; the room is less heated than with a coal fire; and the blaze may be turned out when no longer needed. Already in some parts of the country natural gas is led by pipes directly from the wells into houses for cooking and for heating purposes. Already experiments in heating houses and cooking food by means of electricity are common and to some extent successful. It would seem that the inventions and improvements of the next hundred years may render the homes as much more comfortable than those of to-day as ours surpass those of our ancestors.

THOMAS A. EDISON.

MINOT'S LEDGE LIGHT, MASSACHUSETTS BAY.

SECTION II.
LIGHT.

CHAPTER I.

TORCHES.

Wood and coal, gas and oil, electricity even, aid us in our demand for warm houses. In winter we should suffer greatly were it not for our fireplaces, our stoves, and our furnaces. The sun then shines but a short time every day, and sends us little heat. In summer "the great orb of day" remains many hours in the heavens, and warms us through and through. We have little desire then for artificial heat; natural heat is sometimes more than sufficient.

The sun shines over all the world. "His going forth is from the end of the heaven, and his circuit unto the ends of it: and there is nothing hid from the heat thereof."

The sun does much more for us than send us its heat-rays: all day long we rejoice in the bright sunshine. But at night, when the sun has set, we ask for artificial light. How shall we get it? How did our ancestors obtain it?

INDIANS TRAVELING AT NIGHT.

We have in our day the electric light; we can use illuminating gas; kerosene is easily obtained; if necessary, we can resort to candles. Yet there was a time when the electric light had not been discovered. Earlier still, gas had not been made and kerosene was not known. Indeed, long, long ago even candles had not been seen by men. What did the people do for light on a dark night in those times? After the sun had set and night had settled down upon them, what could they do during the long winter evenings without some method of lighting up the darkness?

As we looked to the American Indians for the simplest and rudest methods of obtaining heat, so we can also learn something from them of the primitive modes of lighting. Much of the time the red men found sufficient light for all their wants in the wood fire. They needed no candles to read by, for they had no books nor papers. They cared for no lamp to dress by; they sought no illumination for halls or churches or theatres. What little need they had for artificial light was practically satisfied by that which came from the blazing logs.

If, however, on any special occasion they wished to light up their long houses more brightly, the Indians used pitch-pine knots. In case they were traveling by night and did not care to proceed stealthily or secretly, these fagots of pitch pine gave them all the light they wanted. The light from these sticks was dim; it flickered so as to hurt the eyes; more smoke was given out than light; but the savage was fully content.

Long before the red men were known, however, the burning fagot was used by the people of Europe and Asia to lessen the darkness of the night.

An interesting story is told of Hannibal when he was leading the Carthaginian army against Rome. In the course of his journey he marched his whole force into a valley which was entirely surrounded by high mountains very difficult to cross. Fabius, his Roman opponent, placed his own army in the pass and enclosed Hannibal in the valley. Hannibal was apparently caught in a trap, but he was a shrewd commander, and he quickly devised a trick to make Fabius withdraw his legions. Early in the day he sent out a large detail from his army to gather fagots. What was he about to do with such great quantities of pine knots?

In the afternoon, by Hannibal's orders, these fagots were bound to the horns of oxen which had been driven along during the march for food for the army. At nightfall the fagots were lighted and the oxen were driven directly up the steep side of one of the mountains. Fabius naturally supposed that the lights moving up the mountain-side must be carried by soldiers, and he thought that Hannibal and all his army were trying to escape in that direction. Accordingly he quickly withdrew his troops from the pass in order to attack the enemy when they came down the opposite side of the mountain. Hannibal then quietly marched his army through the pass, meeting with no opposition.

Long, long centuries before Hannibal the torch was known. In that strange story of Gideon and his three hundred men who overcame the Midianites, the torch or lamp was one of the weapons used. The vast host of the Midianites, fearing no hostile attack, was spread over a great valley. Gideon placed his little band of men on the hills around the enemy's camp, each man at a considerable distance from the next, so that they made a line nearly surrounding the entire valley. Every man had a trumpet in one hand, and a lamp or torch covered by an upturned pitcher in the other. This arrangement of the lamp and the pitcher allowed a little light to be thrown upon the ground directly beneath. The men could thus avoid stepping upon dry sticks and making a noise which might alarm the guards around the camp of the Midianites. At the same time the light was concealed from the eyes of their enemies.

When all was ready a shout was raised, "The sword of the Lord and of Gideon!" and the pitchers were thrown with a great crash upon the ground. The sudden noise of voices and of the breaking pitchers awoke the Midianites from a deep sleep; the trumpets and the shouts turned their eyes to the hills. All along the line of the three hundred men spread out in a circle around them blazed the three hundred torches. As it was the custom in those days to have a torch or a lamp indicate the headquarters of a general, the Midianites in their sudden terror naturally thought that an immense army was surrounding them. They imagined that Gideon had hired vast forces from Egypt and elsewhere, for they supposed that each of the several hundred torches indicated a general with all his followers. Their only thought, therefore, was to flee as quickly as possible. They ran against each other, and, unable in the darkness to distinguish friend from foe, they killed their own men. The entire army of one hundred and thirty-five thousand men perished.

ANCIENT LAMPS.

It is not certain whether the lights which were covered by the pitchers came from lamps or torches. Gideon lived three thousand years ago, and at that time both torches and lamps were used. He was a general of the Israelites, and they certainly had lamps when in Egypt many years before the time of Gideon. Lamps were also used by the Greeks and the Romans.

The lamp of these ancient times was merely a small vessel like a modern cup or bowl, usually having a handle. This was filled with oil, generally olive, or sometimes only with grease. In this cup was placed a small piece of cloth hanging over the side, which when lighted served as a wick. It was the simplest arrangement possible.

The pitch-pine knot and the cup of grease have been more or less used since these early times. When our ancestors came to this country their houses were generally lighted by candles. In many cases, however, the light from the fireplace was all that was used except on rare occasions. The settlers who gradually moved westward to take up new lands retained nearly all the inconvenient methods of the earlier colonists. In the newer settlements of the Ohio and Mississippi valleys and on the great Western plains the logs on the hearth were frequently the only means for lighting the house during the evenings.

On Knob Creek, in the new State of Kentucky, a little school was kept nearly eighty-five years ago. Among the pupils was a small boy not seven years of age. One of his schoolmates afterward said of him that he was "an unusually bright boy at school, and made splendid progress in his studies. He would get spice-wood brushes, hack them up on a log, and burn two or three together for the purpose of giving light by which he might pursue his studies." It does not surprise us to learn that this boy who thus in his earliest years showed such eagerness to learn as to utilize the light of the kitchen fire was Abraham Lincoln, afterward the famous President of the United States.

Many men are now living who do not remember to have seen in their boyhood days any better light than the grease lamp. One of these primitive lamps was easily made. An old button was covered with cloth, which was tied with a string close to the button, the edges of the cloth hanging free. This covered button was placed upon lard in a saucer or other similar vessel, and a light applied. The lard around the cloth melted, the button acted as a wick, and a rude lamp was the result.

The hearth fire, the fagot or pitch-pine knot, and the pot of grease or lard with a simple wick were the earliest methods of artificial lighting. These, though still in use in newly settled communities, gave place, in the main, centuries ago to the candle. As this was the first improved method for lighting houses, churches, and other buildings, it should next be considered.

CHAPTER II.

CANDLES.

Nobody can tell when candles were invented. Candlesticks are often spoken of in the Bible, but those doubtless held oil and burned a wick which hung over the side like the Roman lamps of later time. These lamps appear to have been used by the Romans in their worship, and after the Christian religion was established at Rome, candles were introduced into the Christian service. During all the centuries since that time the candle has been used in Catholic churches and cathedrals.

The Romans on the second day of February burned candles to the goddess Februa, the mother of Mars, the Roman god of war, and Pope Sergius adopted the custom and established rites and ceremonies for that day in the offering of candles to the Virgin Mary. This was called Candlemas day. The common people supposed that these candles would frighten away the devil and all evil spirits not only from the persons who burned them, but from the houses in which they were placed. There is an ancient tradition about Candlemas day which seems to have traveled all over Europe and found its way into this country; if the weather is fine on that day—February 2d—it indicates a long winter and a late spring. The Scotch state the legend in this way:

> "If Candlemas day is fair and clear,
> There'll be two winters in the year."

For several centuries past candles have been used all over the world for lighting purposes. We have a variety of candles even in these days, as they are now made of tallow, stearin, bleached wax, spermaceti, and paraffine. Those commonly used by the early colonists were dipped candles, often roughly made at home. For the wicks a loose, soft, fibrous substance was taken, generally cotton. These were hung upon a frame and dipped in melted tallow, taken out, suffered to cool, and dipped again and again until the required thickness was obtained. Moulded candles were cast in a series of tubes, the wicks first being adjusted in the middle of the tubes and melted tallow poured in. The best candles were made of wax. These were neither dipped nor moulded. The wicks were warmed, and melted wax poured over them until they acquired the proper thickness, then they were rolled between flat pieces of wet, hard wood.

It is related of Benjamin Franklin that when a young man he received an invitation from Gov. William Burnet, of New York, to call upon him. The governor was delighted with his conversation, and was surprised to hear him quote from Locke on the Understanding. The governor asked him at what college he had studied

Locke.

"Why, sir," said Franklin, "it was my misfortune never to be at any college, or even at a grammar school, except for a year or two when I was a child."

Here the governor sprang from his seat, and staring at Ben, cried out: "Well, and where did you get your education, pray?"

"At home, sir, in a tallow-chandler's shop."

"In a tallow-chandler's shop!" exclaimed the governor.

"Yes, sir; my father was a poor old tallow chandler with fifteen children, and I the youngest of all. [His father had, later, two other children, both girls.] At eight he put me to school; but finding he could not spare the money from the rest of the children to keep me there, he took me home into the shop, where I assisted him by twisting candlewicks and filling the moulds all day, and at night read by myself." So Benjamin Franklin spent two years of his life, between the ages of ten and twelve, in making candles for the good people of Boston.

FRANKLIN MAKING CANDLES.

The candles gave but a poor light compared with the lights which we have to-day. The combustion was only partial, and there was constant trouble from the necessity of "snuffing the candle," that is, cutting off the burnt wick. In those days, in every well-regulated house, on the little centre-table stood the candlestick, and by its side upon a small tray made for the purpose could always be found the "snuffers" — a singular instrument, something like a pair of scissors, with a small semi-circular pocket in which to hold the snuff taken from the candle.

READING BY CANDLELIGHT.

Let us imagine an early New England family on a winter's evening sitting before the blazing fire of the open fireplace. They are gathered around a small table upon which is a solitary candle, giving a feeble, sickly flame. By its light the mother is sewing and the father is reading from the Bible, The Pilgrim's Progress, or it may be Bacon's Essays, or Locke on the Understanding. The children are listening and trying to get interested in what is being read to them, while occasionally one or another of them snuffs the little candle. By and by the candle burns down "to the socket," and goes out. The mother rises and goes to the pantry to get another, but finds to her dismay that she has used her last one. The family must therefore see by the light of the fire or retire for the night, and to-morrow the good wife must dip some more candles.

When the children go to bed they have no brightly burning lamp to light them to their several bedrooms, but they climb the ladder to the open, unfinished loft with no light except what comes to them from the embers upon the hearth. Then the father covers up the coals with a great body of ashes, hoping to "keep the fire" till morning. What a marked contrast between the life of those people and the customs of to-day in the same country and among the grandchildren and the great-grandchildren of those same pioneer settlers!

In the colonial days for an evening service the churches must be lighted with candles. Occasionally you will find even now in some ancient church the antique candelabra or chandelier. Sometimes in wealthy churches these were made of glass, and were of beautiful construction. In the old meeting-house of the first Baptist church in Providence, Rhode Island, which was founded by Roger Williams and others in 1639, there is one of these ancient glass candelabras. It is of immense proportions, hanging from the ceiling by a long, stout chain, and arranged for a large number of candles. It has not been used for many years, but it is a beautiful ornament and a suggestive reminder of the method by which our ancestors lighted their churches in the early times.

In these days of brilliant electric lights, how small appears the light of the ancient candles! Have we gained in knowledge and manner of living as greatly as in heating and lighting our houses?

CHAPTER III.

WHALE OIL.

No one knows when the whale fishery began. Eight hundred years ago whales were caught off the coast of France and Spain, and before the Pilgrim fathers landed at Plymouth the whale fishery had been carried on to such an extent on the west coast of Europe that the supply of whales had begun to fail. The American whale fishery began with the earliest settlers. They found it profitable to catch whales and try out the oil for use in their lamps. It has been said that one of the arguments for settling on Cape Cod was the presence along the coast of large whales of the best kind for oil and whalebone.

The first whale fishery in America was carried on from Cape Cod, Nantucket, and Martha's Vineyard by large rowboats. A company of hardy pioneers would row out from the coast into deep water, wait for the appearance of a whale, strike their harpoons into his side, and let him run. Sometimes it would be days before death would result. Often he would sink and later rise and float upon the surface. The fishermen would then pull him to the shore and try out the oil. Many whales thus harpooned would be lost to those who had wounded them. A story is told that in the town of Southampton, Long Island, before the year 1650, the men divided themselves into squads to watch night and day for whales that might come ashore, and this became in a few years a regular industry.

After a time whaling vessels were fitted up and sent out for the capture of whales. These vessels cruised in all waters. They coasted along Greenland and into the Arctic Ocean. They traversed the South Seas, and sailed upon the Pacific through all latitudes from Patagonia to Bering Sea. Great vessels—barks, brigs, and full-rigged ships—manned with large crews of stalwart men, with supplies for a three-years' voyage or more, would leave home for a cruise in foreign waters after these monsters of the deep.

When the whale is killed its body is towed alongside the vessel and is made fast by the ship's chains. The fat of the whale is cut into slices, and these slices taken in between decks. This cutting up—or, as the sailors call it, "cutting in"—occupies the entire ship's company for hours. The fat or "blubber," as they call it, is cut into smaller cubical pieces, heated in a large pot, and the oil strained off. This is called "trying out." The oil is stored in casks to be conveyed home. A large whale will give two or three tons of blubber. It is estimated that a ton of blubber will yield nearly two hundred gallons of oil. Sometimes a single whale will produce oil and whalebone to the value of $3,000 or $4,000.

WHALE FISHING.

It will readily be seen that whale fishing is both a laborious and a dangerous occupation. The wounded whale is accustomed to strike violently with its tail in the endeavor to destroy its enemies. Here is a true story about the experiences of one family engaged in the whale fishery. Long before the year 1800 and after that date for almost half a century, New Bedford, Nantucket, Martha's Vineyard, and Provincetown in Massachusetts, with Warren and Bristol in Rhode Island, engaged very largely in this hazardous but profitable business. In one of these towns an industrious and enterprising man of more than ordinary ability followed this occupation for half a century and amassed a small fortune. He had several sons. When the oldest grew to manhood he very naturally followed in the footsteps of his father. He went to sea on a whaling vessel and was lost during his first voyage.

The second son shipped on a whaler. In the Arctic waters he was one day pursuing a whale that had already been wounded, rowing with all his might. The whale in his anger struck at the boat with his huge tail, hit the oar with which the young man was rowing, and drove the end of it into his mouth, breaking the bones and crushing in the very interior. Still the young man lived. He was tenderly cared for by his shipmates, and finally reached home. Then he was turned over to the doctors. Skillful surgery supplied him with a false lower jaw, a gold roof to his mouth, and a false palate. He lived many years and was a successful business man. Had you met him on the street he would have talked with you like any other man, and you would have observed nothing unusual except the scars of two cuts on the upper lip.

The third son when eighteen years of age also left home on a whaling voyage. At the end of three years his ship returned with a full cargo of excellent oil. The heavily freighted vessel anchored in the bay, and the captain went up to the town in a rowboat to announce his arrival, and to tell the people of the success of the voyage and that all were well on board. Just as the captain was leaving for the shore some young men in the crew, wishing to celebrate their safe return, proposed firing the ship's swivel-gun. As the captain started over the side of the vessel he cautioned them, saying that the gun was rusty and that it would not be safe to fire it. But it was our young friend's birthday. He would risk the old gun. They ran it out on deck, loaded it up, and touched it off. There was a terrific explosion. The gun burst and blew off both hands of the young man who was celebrating his birthday. Another boat was pushed off for the shore and carried the wounded man to his home. Nothing could save his hands; they were both amputated at the wrists. Through a long life he wore wooden hands covered with kid gloves. He was accustomed frequently to mourn that he had not at least one thumb. If he could have had a single thumb he could have done many things. Was it not Emerson who said that the thumb is the symbol of civilization? Man could never have attained his present position without a thumb.

For many years this man, thus maimed for life, kept a store and sold groceries and ship supplies. A visitor one day saw him weigh out for a lady customer a quarter of a pound of pepper. It was at the noon hour, when the clerks were all away at dinner. The customer came and asked for a quarter of a pound of pepper. The storekeeper pulled out the drawer, placed it on the counter, put a piece of paper in the hopper, adjusted the scale to the quarter pound, slipped one of his wooden fingers through the handle of the little tin scoop, and scattered the pepper upon the paper until the full weight was made. He then returned the drawer to its place, took off the hopper and laid it upon the counter, pulled out the paper and the pepper, doubled the paper over on one side and back from the other side, doubled over one end and then the other, picked it up between his two wooden hands, and handed it to the customer. She placed the money on the back of his hand. With the other hand he pulled open the money drawer and tossed the money in. With both hands he took off his hat, picked up the change with his lips, placed the change upon the back of his hand, and passed it to the lady. Three unfortunate experiences in one family would seem to have been enough, so the next son never went to sea.

We may now ask what was the object of all this whale fishery? Man had made a new invention. He had not only discovered the value of whale oil as a material for furnishing artificial light, he had also invented the modern lamp. In the candle the burning material, whether tallow or something else, is solidified around the wick. The heat from the burning wick melts the tallow and the combustion gives light.

In the modern lamp the simple device of a tube or two tubes to hold the wick is all that is needed over and above those used in ancient times. Tin tubes are placed in the top of the lamp and the wicks run up through the tubes. The lamp then being filled with oil, capillary attraction will bring the oil up to the top of the wick. The lamp when lighted will burn until the supply of oil is exhausted.

The invention of this modern lamp, though very simple, has been of great value. At first it was made of metal—lead, block tin, Britannia, brass—and finally of glass. Lamps of various patterns and different sizes became common. For a long while very little change was made in this new mode of obtaining light. This method continued in common use until about the middle of the nineteenth century.

CHAPTER IV.

KEROSENE.

IT was a long step from the smoky and ill-smelling whale-oil lamp to the clear and brilliant kerosene burner. At the present time the best illumination is furnished by gas and electricity, but in the country and to a large extent in the cities the kerosene lamp is still in common use, and doubtless will remain so for a long time to come. This lamp with its recent important improvements is mainly of American origin and development.

Kerosene for lighting purposes has some advantages over gas or electricity. The light produced from it is steady; therefore it is less harmful to the eyes than the flickering light of illuminating gas, and even better than the electric light. It is far cheaper than either. It has a third advantage, since it can be used in a hand lamp which can be carried from place to place. A large portion of our population consider it so valuable that they would rather give up the gaslight altogether, or indeed the electric light, than be obliged to lose the kerosene lamp.

Kerosene is a form of petroleum which is obtained from the earth by deep wells. It is only within the last fifty years that this oil has been pumped in sufficient quantities to make it a valuable industry, though petroleum was obtained here and there in small quantities far back in the early ages. It seems a little singular that the people of Japan and Persia should have dug oil wells centuries ago. Herodotus, who wrote history five hundred years before Christ, tells us of the springs of Zante, one of the Ionian Islands in the Mediterranean Sea, from which oil flowed. It is said that these springs are still flowing.

China seems to have been the first country to draw oil from artesian wells. We proud Americans are accustomed to think ourselves a little ahead of all other people. When an American boy in San Francisco, for instance, meets a Chinese lad, he is quite apt to look down upon him and to think that this little Chinese boy came from a country hardly civilized and certainly far behind the "universal Yankee nation;" yet we are constantly finding traces of a civilization in China much earlier than our own.

The first successful oil well in this country was made by Col. E. L. Drake, near Titusville, Pennsylvania. In 1854 the Pennsylvania Rock-Oil Company was organized for the purpose of procuring petroleum in Oil Creek. Four years later this company employed Colonel Drake to drill an artesian well. On the 29th of August, 1859, he "struck oil" only sixty-nine feet below the surface of the ground. The next day this well was found to be nearly full of petroleum.

Oil is now found in large quantities in various sections of Pennsylvania, New York, Indiana, and Kentucky, and it has recently been discovered in California, Wyoming, Colorado, and other portions of our land. The largest part of the oil used in commerce is from Pennsylvania. At the present time more than fifty million barrels of petroleum are produced annually in the United States alone, which is more than half of the entire product of the world. A single well has been known to yield forty thousand gallons a day, flowing freely without the slightest use of pumping apparatus.

The product of these wells after a time greatly diminishes and sometimes ceases altogether. In such cases it is customary to explode torpedoes at the bottom of the well. This is done by placing there several gallons of nitroglycerine with a fulminating cap on top. This cap is exploded by dropping a piece of iron upon it. The explosion opens the seams and crevices around the bottom of the well so as to renew the flow of oil.

OIL WELLS.

It is now about forty years since the first introduction of kerosene as an article of commerce. To-day it is in almost universal use throughout the civilized world. It gives a convenient light at a moderate expense, and has therefore proved a great blessing to mankind. Meantime the whale fishery has largely diminished; indeed, it would seem to be almost destroyed. The reasons for this are not difficult to find. In the first place, the number of whales is much less than formerly, so that this business is far less profitable than it used to be. In the second place, the rapid development of the kerosene industry has so cheapened the product that people cannot afford to light their houses with whale oil, especially as they find the kerosene not only cheaper, but more convenient and satisfactory.

Common whale oil previous to 1850 had been furnished at an average cost of perhaps fifty cents a gallon, while the sperm oil, which is of superior quality, cost as much as one dollar a gallon. The people of the whole country east of the Rocky Mountains feed their lamps to-day with kerosene at a cost of from eight cents to twelve cents a gallon.

A few persons have made great fortunes from the oil wells. On the other hand, it should not be forgotten that the modern processes of purifying kerosene could not have been put in operation without the aid of large fortunes. A cheap and satisfactory light has been furnished to all the people of the United States only by means of the great capital employed in its production.

So you see civilization is progressing, and we are all enjoying more blessings and conveniences than our fathers had. In the earlier times every one had to labor diligently to secure food, clothing, and shelter. As civilization advances these require less time and expense, and we have greater opportunities to attend to the development of our higher natures, the acquisition of knowledge, the pursuit of science, and the elevation of the race.

CHAPTER V.

ILLUMINATING GAS.

Thus far our various methods of artificial lighting have been very simple. At first men burned the pitch from the pine, and it produced a flame; then they burned olive oil through a wick, and it gave forth a flame. The tallow in the candle was burned through a wick, and it made a light; the whale oil in the lamp was burned by means of a wick, and a light was the result. In the same way refined petroleum, which we call kerosene, was burned by means of a wick, and that gave a strong light. These methods of lighting were all very similar.

We come now to a real invention. What would a boy of the year 1800, could he return to the earth, say to see you strike a match, turn a stopcock, and light the gas as you do to-day? He has never seen a match. He is just as ignorant of a stopcock, and surely it would be difficult for him to understand the burning of the gas. Many things would need to be explained to this boy of a hundred years ago. He must be told all about the production of illuminating gas, the storing of that gas under pressure, the transportation of it to the place where the light is wanted, and the proper apparatus for turning it on, setting it on fire, and regulating its pressure so as to produce a steady, uniform light.

Before the year 1700 Dr. John Clayton, an Englishman, prepared gas from bituminous coal, collected it, and burned it for the amusement of his friends. An English bishop in 1767 showed how gas could be produced from coal and how it might be conveyed in tubes. These were the first two steps toward our present almost universal illumination by gas: making gas and conveying it in tubes.

The real inventor of practical gas-lighting was William Murdoch, of Cornwall, England, who sometime before the year 1800 carried pipes through his house and office, and lighted the various rooms with gas which he had made from coal. Indeed, Murdoch did more than this: he lighted with his new gas a small steam carriage in which he rode to and from his mines. In 1802 he first publicly exhibited this gas-lighting in Ayrshire, Scotland, and showed two immense flames from coal gas. Nor did he stop here, for in 1805 he succeeded in lighting some cotton mills by the same method.

In our country various experiments were made, but without any practical result until 1821, when illuminating gas was successfully manufactured and used in Baltimore. In 1827 the New York Gaslight Company introduced this new method into many houses and sold the gas to the people for lighting purposes.

That was over seventy years ago. What a change has been made within these seventy years! In cities and large towns almost every new house is piped for gas. Gas companies are formed for supplying this illuminating product to the inhabitants. Gas meters have been perfected which measure the quantity of gas, so that one pays for no more than he uses. Moreover, the towns and cities put up street lights which burn this same gas in the night, making it easy, convenient, and safe to traverse the streets at any hour.

Bituminous or soft coal is used in the manufacture of illuminating gas, as anthracite contains less of the needed materials. Gases are easily driven off from bituminous coal whenever it is heated, if air is kept from it. At the works, therefore, the coal is placed in large closed ovens, called *retorts*. These are directly over furnace fires, which are kept vigorously burning. The gases pass out of the coal and, rising, enter a series of long pipes. The coal which is left in the retorts is called coke. This process is called *distillation*.

A GASOMETER.

Many substances pass off with the gas, from which it must be cleaned. Tar and ammonia become liquids when cooled, and are left behind as the gas passes through cold water. The series of iron pipes in which this process is carried on is called the *condenser*. Then the gas is carried through the *purifier*, in which all other impurities are removed.

When thoroughly purified the gas passes into the *gasometer*. This usually consists of two round iron cylinders of nearly the same size, one inside of the other. The outside cylinder has no roof; the inside has no floor. The sides of the inner one go down into a trench filled with water. Its top is held up by the gas, which comes into it from the purifier.

The roof of the inner cylinder presses down heavily upon the gas, pushing it into the large *main pipes*, which run from the gasometer through the principal streets. Smaller mains connect with these and the gas is pushed into the *service pipes*, which enter the houses. When a stopcock is opened in any house the pressure of the gasometer pushes the gas through, it may be, miles of pipes, and out through the burner, where it may be lighted.

Many houses have a simple electric-lighting attachment, so that by merely turning a stopcock the gas is turned on and by pulling a chain an electric spark sets the gas on fire, flooding the room with light.

Within a few years illuminating gas has greatly diminished in price. It costs a little more than kerosene, but it is more convenient in many ways. The danger of carrying lamps from room to room is avoided, as well as the disagreeable task of filling them. Still the gas flame is less steady than that of the kerosene lamp, and is therefore less serviceable for reading. For the poor man the kerosene light is a great blessing, while for all who can afford the extra cost the gaslight is a greater convenience.

CHAPTER VI.
ELECTRIC LIGHTING.

THE electric light differs widely from all modes of artificial light previously invented. It is the latest method that man has discovered for the production of light. In its practical form this invention is quite recent. In England the arc light was produced in lecture-room experiments as early as 1802. Prof. Michael Faraday, a learned Englishman and celebrated chemist, experimented many years in electricity and magnetism in the Royal Institution at London. He continued his studies and experiments in developing the science of electricity through his whole life, but he died, an old man, before a single electric arc was seen in the streets of London.

In ancient times an invention was frequently the result of one man's efforts, but at the present time it is often quite otherwise. Many men are now engaged in the development of electric lighting. Charles Francis Brush was a farmer's boy in Ohio. He pushed himself through the Cleveland High School and graduated at the University of Michigan. He established a laboratory in Cleveland and turned his attention to the invention of apparatus for electric lighting. He was one of three or four great American inventors who successfully put into operation the dynamo and furnished electricity for the electrical lamp. This dynamo is a machine which produces electric currents by mechanical power. Brush's dynamo at the outset was so perfect and complete that for many years it has continued in regular use with but very little change.

Elihu Thomson graduated at the Central High School in Philadelphia and taught chemistry in that school. He studied with great care the subject of electricity, giving special attention to lighting. He organized the Thomson-Houston Electric Company, and has patented nearly two hundred inventions relating to electric lighting and other applications of electricity. He was also the inventor of the system of electric welding.

Among the great American inventors in electrical science is Thomas Alva Edison. He was an Ohio boy whose Scotch mother taught him to read. When he was twelve years old he was a newsboy on the Grand Trunk Railroad. Here he acquired the habit of reading. He studied chemistry and conducted chemical experiments on the train. He learned to set type, and edited and printed a newspaper in the baggage car. He was constantly noticing the telegraph stations along the road, and he soon began to study electricity.

One day the little child of a station master was playing on the track just as a freight car was moving down toward him. Almost as swift as lightning itself young Edison dashed out, stepped in front of the coming car, and at the risk of his own life snatched the child from danger. In gratitude the station master, knowing the boy's interest in the telegraph, taught him how to use a machine. After that he acquired great skill in this art and operated in many sections of the country, perfecting himself in the subject.

EDISON'S HEROIC ACT.

For over twenty years he has had a large establishment, with an immense workshop and many mechanics, at Menlo Park, N. J., where he has devoted his whole attention to inventing. He has perfected his system of duplex telegraphy and invented the carbon telephone-transmitter, the phonograph, the platinum burner, and the carbon burner for the incandescent light. He has patented very many inventions, and his system of electric lighting for houses is now in general use. Edison's whole life is an interesting study for young people.

At the present time the two methods of lighting by electricity are the arc light and the incandescent light. The arc light is used for lighting large buildings like churches, halls, and railway stations, and for lighting the streets of a city. The incandescent light, or the glow-lamp as it is called in England, is in general use for lighting dwelling houses. This lamp consists of a glass bulb from which air has been excluded so that it is almost a perfect vacuum and in which is inserted a looped filament of carbon. The electricity is made to pass through this carbon wire, which is thereby heated to a white heat and thus furnishes the light. Being in a vacuum, the carbon is but slightly burned. It therefore can be subjected to this heat for a long time without breaking or wearing out.

At first Edison used a platinum wire in the little electric lamp. He wanted something better. He needed some form of bamboo or other vegetable fibre. He sent a man to explore China and Japan for bamboo. He sent another, who traveled twenty-three hundred miles up the Amazon River and finally reached the Pacific coast, searching for bamboo. He sent a third to Ceylon to spend years in a similar search. Eighty varieties of bamboo and three thousand specimens of other vegetable fibre were brought him. He tested them all; three or four were found suitable.

This system of incandescent lights has been rapidly extended within a few years. There are millions of these lights now in use in this country. They are used not only for lighting the rooms of hotels and private houses, but also for lighting steamships, railway trains, and street cars, and for nearly all indoor illumination. This light is not as cheap as kerosene or gaslight, but it is so convenient and so simple, requiring no daily care, that it is rapidly coming into use in all towns and cities.

Among its advantages may be named the four following points. Matches are not needed in making a light. Thus the danger from accidental fires, which have so frequently occurred from the careless use of matches, is avoided. Very little heat results from an electric light, while from kerosene lamps and gaslight much heat is produced. In warm weather this freedom from heat is agreeable. The burning lamp and the gas jet make the air of the room impure and unfit for breathing. This is not true of the electric light. In the use of kerosene and of illuminating gas there is frequently danger of explosion. Not so with the electric light.

It will be seen that we are thus using to-day for lighting purposes occasionally the candle, quite largely the kerosene lamp, and to a great extent in towns and cities the gaslight, and best of all—the cleanest, the neatest, giving the brightest light, requiring the least attention from the consumer, and manifesting the highest development of man's inventive genius thus far—the electric light. Here at present man's invention in this direction has stopped. What the next step will be, no one can tell.

Slowly through the ages man has been developing. Gradually he has grown in mental power and advanced morally and spiritually. It is very clear that although he is an animal and has the nature and desires of an animal, he has high mental capacity and is endowed with a spiritual nature, a soul. At the very beginning of creation we are told, "God said, Let there be light: and there was light." How and whence it came we cannot tell. It would almost seem that man in his effort to create light has kept step with his own development. The first light was produced from the simplest substances, solids: wood on the hearth, the pitch-pine knot, and the candle. Then followed light produced from liquids: olive oil, whale oil, refined petroleum. Afterward the inventive genius of man extracted from coal an invisible gas which would burn and give a bright, clear light. Rising higher and higher, man soars above all solids, liquids, and gases, and with a sudden bound leaps almost out of the realm of matter and produces the electric light, which is merely a form of motion. How clearly the progress of man, his elevation, his civilization, his increased conveniences and luxuries of life are made to appear in this study of his methods of obtaining artificial light!

CHAPTER VII.
LIGHTHOUSES.

WE have seen that artificial light is needed at night not only in houses, churches, and public halls, but also in the streets of large towns and cities for the benefit of those who have occasion to travel after dark. Still further, it has been found necessary to light the shores of the great sea, so that vessels may not run upon the rocks in the darkness and be stove to pieces.

The building of lighthouses has chiefly developed during the present century, although a few lighthouses were known to the ancients. The full history of lighthouses, if we could trace it, would be very interesting. If you were asked where the first lighthouse was built you would be quite likely to guess right the first time, because you know that the first ships and the first sailors were around the eastern part of the Mediterranean Sea. You would certainly say somewhere along the eastern coast of that sea. Now as a matter of fact there was a lighthouse on the island of Pharos, just in front of the city of Alexandria, which was built over three hundred years before Christ. This was one of the most celebrated towers of antiquity; in fact, it is classed among the Seven Wonders of the World. It is quite likely, however, that this was not the first lighthouse. Probably there were towers on the Dardanelles, the Sea of Marmora, and the Bosphorus which may have preceded the Pharos of Alexandria.

The Romans built lighthouses at Ostia, Ravenna, Puteoli, and other ports. All these ancient lighthouses were towers on the top of which wood was burned at night, and the blaze of the burning wood furnished the light which was to guide the mariner.

Two or three centuries ago many lighthouses were built along the shores of France and England. The first lighthouse on the coast of our country was Boston Light, at the entrance to Boston harbor, which was erected in the year 1716. Ever since the United States government has been established, much attention has been paid to our system of lighthouses. In 1852 a lighthouse board was established within the department of the United States Treasury.

Great skill and engineering ability are needed in the construction of lighthouses. Our country has long Atlantic, Pacific, and lake coasts to be protected, besides numerous rivers extending over thousands of miles. All along these coasts and rivers our government has established and maintains lighthouses. We have nearly a thousand lights on the Atlantic coast, nearly two hundred upon the Pacific, and several hundred along the shores of the Northern Lakes. The United States has also many fog signals and almost innumerable buoys. Great sums of money are necessary to build these lighthouses, many of which are now of iron. Twelve of our most famous lighthouses have cost a total sum of upward of $3,000,000 for their construction. Each year witnesses a steady improvement in the method of construction and of lighting this multitude of lighthouses.

At first, fires burning at the tops of lighthouses were the only signals and guides at night. Then came the use of oil in lamps, with reflectors constructed for the purpose. At first in this country fish oil was used, and after that sperm oil. Within the last ten years refined petroleum has been almost universally adopted for lighthouses in the United States. At present about a million gallons are used in a year. We have only a few electric lights, though two are now in use on the Atlantic coast and two or three upon the lakes.

In late years commerce has been rapidly extended. The merchant marine of the nations has grown to gigantic proportions. The amount of travel not only coastwise but across the ocean for pleasure and profit has become enormous. The nations are coming closer together and becoming better acquainted with each other. All this promotes civilization, and will ere long, it is to be hoped, operate to prevent international wars.

England has many famous lighthouses. Great Britain is an island and her coast shows a continuous series of indentations. Perhaps the most famous of her lighthouses is the Eddystone Light, a few miles off from Plymouth.

If you will look on your map of Great Britain you will find that the county of Northumberland is the extreme northern end of England, bordering on the North Sea and adjoining the southeast corner of Scotland. Off that coast you will see a little group of islands called the Farne Islands. At low tide there are twenty-five of them. On one of these little islands, early in the present century, stood the Longstone Lighthouse. It was a solitary place, and sometimes weeks would pass without any communication with the mainland. The keeper of this light was William Darling, a man of intelligence, who gave a fair education to each of his large family of children. One of these was a daughter whose name was Grace. Think what the youth of an intelligent girl would be on one of the Farne Islands. They are extremely desolate, are covered with rocks, and have very little vegetation and very little animal life except sea fowl.

Through the channels between these islands the sea rushes with great force, and many a brave ship has gone down, dashed to pieces upon the rocks. In 1838 a large steamer named the *Forfarshire* struck these rocks and was broken in two within sight of Longstone Lighthouse. This steamer had on board more than forty passengers and twenty officers and crew. Three persons only were in the lighthouse—Mr. Darling, his wife, and Grace. The storm was furious, the sea was running high, and through the mist, with the aid of his glass, Mr. Darling could make out the figures of the sufferers who were still clinging to the broken vessel. The lighthouse-keeper shrank from attempting their rescue, but Grace insisted that they must make the effort to save them from certain death. Even the launching of the boat was extremely hazardous. The old lighthouse-keeper thought it impossible, but he could not resist the pleadings of his daughter. The mother helped to launch the boat; the father and daughter entered it and each took an oar. It was a terrible undertaking to row the frail boat, and it required not only great muscular power but the most determined courage.

The rescuers succeeded in reaching the rocks, but found great difficulty in steadying the boat to prevent it from being destroyed on the sharp ridges. There were nine persons clinging to the broken vessel. These nine were all rescued. By tremendous energy, great skill, and almost superhuman efforts they were rowed back to the lighthouse in safety.

This heroic deed of a young woman scarcely twenty-three years of age was heralded abroad until she became well known all over Europe, and the lonely lighthouse was soon the centre of attraction to thousands of curious and sympathizing persons. The Humane Society sent her a most flattering vote of thanks, and a public subscription was raised amounting to about thirty-five hundred dollars. Testimonials of all kinds were showered upon her, which produced in her mind only a sense of wonder and grateful pleasure.

GRACE DARLING.

This brief outline of Grace Darling is here given because her heroism served to call the attention of the world to the importance of lighthouses and the isolated life of the keepers and their families. You will find a picturesque account of the life of Grace Darling in the first volume of Chambers's "Miscellany." This story does not stand alone in lighthouse annals, but again and again has it been matched in later times and in our own country.

One of the most famous lighthouse heroines in America was Miss Ida Lewis, whose father kept the Limestone Lighthouse at the entrance to the harbor of Newport, R. I. This lighthouse-keeper's daughter very early in life became skilled in rowing and swimming. One day, when she was eighteen years of age, four young men were upset in a boat in the harbor. Ida quickly launched her own skiff, pushed off, rescued them, and brought them safely to shore.

At another time three drunken soldiers had stove a hole in their boat not far from the lighthouse. Two swam ashore and Ida reached their boat in season to save the third. Two years afterward a sheep was being driven down the wharf when the animal plunged into the water. Three men running along the shore in pursuit found a boat and pushed out after the sheep. A heavy "sou'wester" was blowing and the boat was carried away into deep water. Ida Lewis, in spite of the high wind, rowed out in her little skiff and brought them safely ashore.

One winter a young scapegrace stole a sailboat from the wharf and put out to sea. About midnight the gale drove the boat upon the Limestone rocks a mile from the light, but the boy clung to the mast all night. In the morning Ida Lewis found him, as she said, "shaking and God-blessing me and praying to be set on shore." By these and other instances in which Miss Lewis rescued those in danger she became famous, and her praises were heralded in the newspapers and spoken at many firesides. The citizens of Newport presented her with a boat as a token of their admiration of her bravery.

These famous instances and many more that could be added to them would seem to indicate that life in a lighthouse, with the mind constantly running out to the sea, becoming familiar with the storms that rise, and observing the dash of the waves and the roar of the wind—life inured to hardship, but shut up within the safe keeping of the solid walls of the little tower high above the raging waves—it would seem that such a life is calculated to give courage, strength, and fortitude, and to endue the heart with a heroic forgetfulness of self.

How important is the position of a lighthouse-keeper! Many lives are in his hands, and on his fidelity depends the safety of millions of dollars of property. Boats and ships of all kinds, steamers great and small, sail away from one shore of the vast sea to the opposite shore, or along the coast, all in comparative safety because of the various beacon lights.

Indeed, is not the lighthouse itself a great lesson in morals? Every one of us—every one of the seventy million people of the United States has a part in the lighthouse. It is we, the people, who are furnishing the government with its resources, and it is the great government of our country that builds the lighthouses to warn mariners of danger. The modern lighthouse is the symbol of benevolence. It carries with it the lesson of "loving thy neighbor as thyself." This is the lesson of the lighthouse to the people of the land, though its service is performed for the people of the sea.

CYRUS H. MCCORMICK.

CUTTING SUGAR CANE IN THE HAWAIIAN ISLANDS.

SECTION III.
FOOD.

CHAPTER I.
UNCULTIVATED FOODS.

HEAT and light—each is necessary for our bodily comfort and well-being. We have seen that much time and thought have been spent during the past three hundred years in providing the most satisfactory methods for heating and lighting our houses. We have found that wood and coal in our fireplaces, stoves, and furnaces have given us the best heat. We have learned that kerosene and gas made from coal are the most common sources of light. Even electricity, the latest means for producing light and heat, usually needs the power of steam for its development; and heat is necessary to produce steam. We have a common name for the wood, the coal, the gas, and the oil, from the burning of which heat and light result; this name is fuel.

Another form of fuel is even more necessary than coal and wood. In the winter we warm our rooms so that we may not suffer from the cold; but the stove does not warm us when out of doors. Then we put on our heavy winter wraps, but these give us no warmth: they merely keep in the heat of the body or keep out the cold blasts of the wind. We all know that the body is warm of itself; that there is something within us that produces heat, like a fire. When our fingers become chilled by the frosty air we may warm them with our breath. The temperature of a room may be seventy degrees or less, but if we place the bulb of a thermometer beneath the tongue we shall find that the mercury rises to ninety-eight degrees.

The fire in the body and the fire in the stove act very much alike. If the draughts of the stove are closed tight and no air is admitted, the fire dies down and goes out. If the air which enters the body is foul, the fire feels the effect and our health is injured. If the lungs are filled with water or anything else which keeps out the air, the fire goes out and life is lost.

The fuel which we call food is just as necessary for the fire in our body as is wood or coal for the fire in the stove. Three times a day or oftener we take this food-fuel into our bodies; thus we keep the fire steadily burning which makes us warm and keeps us alive.

On the other hand, fuel for the body must be very different from fuel for a stove. In the stove heat alone is wanted; therefore one form of fuel is enough. In the body bones must be enlarged and strengthened, muscles must be developed, fat must be provided in sufficient quantities, and brain-matter must be produced. Therefore the food-fuel must provide not only heat but also the different materials of which the body is made. One kind of food is necessary for the bones, another for the blood, another for the flesh, and another for the nerves. Thus while in studying common fuel we have only to learn about wood, either in the form of trees or pressed into the form of coal, in studying food-fuel we find that the kinds are almost numberless. Meat and vegetables, fish and fruit, roots and nuts, in their infinite varieties, are all included in the word food.

We are told that all matter belongs to one of three kingdoms—the animal, the vegetable, and the mineral kingdoms. From two of these three divisions we obtain most of our food. Food may be divided into two classes then—animal food and vegetable food. In animal food we have the meat of wild animals and of domestic animals. In early days, when the number of people was small, the supply of wild animals was large. A great part of the food in those days was obtained by hunting and fishing. To-day most of the meat comes from domestic animals, so that the keeping of herds and flocks is one of the great industries of the time. Fish are still important in our lists of foods, but the flesh of wild animals is less and less used for meat.

Three hundred years ago the Indians had this country to themselves. They were few in number and were scattered over a vast territory. The forests abounded in wild game and the lakes and rivers were filled with fish. Love of hunting and fishing held the first place in the pleasures of the red man. The hunting grounds extended far and wide in every direction. Each tribe had its own hunting and fishing grounds, and it was considered an act of war for any tribe of Indians to encroach upon the territory of other tribes.

"Such places as they chose for their abode," says Hubbard's History, "were usually at the falls of great rivers, or near the seaside, where was any convenience for catching such fish as every summer and winter used to come up the coast. At such times they used, like good fellows, to make all common, and then those who had entertained their neighbors at the seaside expected the like kindness from them again up higher in the country."

The kinds of wild animals that the Indians hunted were very numerous. One man describes the appearance of an Indian's "room of skins." He says: "There they showed me many hides and horns, both beasts of chase of the stinking foot—such as roes, foxes, jackals, wolves, wildcats, raccoons, porcupines, skunks, muskrats, squirrels, and sables—and beasts of chase of the sweet foot—buck, red deer, reindeer, moose, bear, beaver, otter, hare, and martin." Captain John Smith tells of the fowl that the red men hunted. He mentions eagles, hawks, cranes, geese, ducks, sheldrakes, teal, gulls, and turkeys.

The variety of fish caught by the Indians was also very large. "Higher up at the falls of the great rivers they used to take salmon, shad, and alewives, that used in great quantities, more than cartloads, in the spring, to pass up into the fresh-water ponds and lakes." "In March, April, May, and half June," says John Smith, "here is cod in abundance; in May, June, July, and August, mullet and sturgeon; herring, if any desire them; I have taken many." Again he writes of whales, grampuses, hake, haddock, mackerel, sharks, cunners, bass, perch, eels, crabs, lobsters, mussels, and oysters.

INDIANS HUNTING GAME.

We may also divide vegetable food into two classes—that which nature provides without the aid of man, or wild vegetables, and that which requires cultivation, or cultivated vegetables. Many forms of nuts, berries and fruits, and some forms of common ground vegetables grow wild. The red men found these in great abundance.

John Smith found in New England currants, mulberries, gooseberries, plums, walnuts, chestnuts, and strawberries, besides other fruits of which he did not know the names. He made a journey up the Potomac River, and reported that the hills yielded no less plenty and variety of fruit than the river furnished abundance of fish.

Smith also described acorns whose bark was white and sweetish; he added that these acorns, when boiled, afforded a sweet oil that the red men kept in gourds to anoint their heads and joints. The Indians also ate the fruit of this acorn, made into bread. There were plums of three kinds and cherries. Smith discovered also a great abundance of vines "that climb the tops of the highest trees in some places. Where they are not overshadowed from the sun, they are covered with fruit, though never pruned nor manured."

Hunting and fishing are carried on in much the same way to-day as they were centuries ago. The gun has taken the place of the bow and arrow, and fishing implements have been somewhat improved. But to capture and kill is now, as formerly, all that is needed to obtain this form of food, if the wild animals themselves can be found. Wild vegetables may be gathered to-day in just the way that our ancestors gathered them, though they are not found in so great quantities because of the increase of cultivation. In studying the changes in the modes of living that have occurred in this country during the last three hundred years, we find that almost all the improvements in the production of food have been in the planting, cultivating, and harvesting of food, and the bringing it to market.

CHAPTER II.
CULTIVATED FOODS.

Hunting and fishing did not furnish either sufficient or satisfactory food for the Indians. A portion of their time was spent in cultivating certain products of the soil. Black Hawk, a famous Indian chief, writes: "When we returned to our village in the spring from our hunting grounds we would open the caches and take out corn and other provisions which had been put up in the fall, and then commence repairing our lodges. As soon as this is accomplished we repair the fences around our fields and clean them off ready for planting corn. This work is done by our women. The men, during this time, are feasting on dried venison, bear's meat, wild fowl and corn.

THE CORN DANCE.

"Our women plant the corn, and as soon as they get done we make a feast and dance the corn dance. At this feast our young braves select the young woman they wish to have for a wife. When this is over we feast again and have our national dance.

"When our national dance is over, our corn-fields hoed, and every weed dug up, and our corn about knee high, all our young men would start in a direction toward sundown to hunt deer and buffalo, and the remainder of our people start to fish. Every one leaves the village and remains away about forty days. They then return, the hunting party bringing in dried buffalo and deer meat, the others dried fish.

"This is a happy season of the year; having plenty of provision, such as beans, squashes, and other produce, with our dried meat and fish, we continue to make feasts and visit each other until our corn is ripe.

"When the corn is fit for use another great ceremony takes place, with feasting and returning thanks to the Great Spirit for giving us corn. We continue our sport and feasting until the corn is all secured. We then prepare to leave our village for our hunting grounds."

Thus we see that the most important crop among the Indians was maize or Indian corn. This grain is specially suited to the climate and soil of a large portion of the country; it was wholly unknown to the Europeans who first came to America.

John Smith in Virginia and Roger Williams in New England were much interested in the Indian corn. It is from their writings that we learn how the red men cultivated and used this strange product of the New World.

As corn was the Indians' main dependence, they ate it at all times and in various ways. They roasted the green ears in the ashes; sometimes they cut the kernels from the cob and boiled them with beans, making a kind of succotash. Meal was made by pounding the kernels in a wooden mortar; if the corn was old it was soaked over night and pounded in the morning.

This meal also was cooked in different ways. Sometimes it was wrapped in corn husks and boiled; at other times it was mixed with water and made into cakes, which were baked in the ashes of the fire. Often a pudding was made from the meal, in which blackberries were placed. When the Indians travelled, they were accustomed to carry enough of this meal to last several days, either in a small basket or a hollow leathern girdle.

Such was life among the Indians. Usually food was plenty and feasting was common, but at times food was scarce and fasting was necessary. If the Indian had sufficient for to-day, he cared little for to-morrow. If the corn crop failed or if the hunting expedition turned out badly, the red man accepted it as a necessary evil and made no complaint.

The first Englishmen to learn of the foods that could be obtained in the New World were two captains sent out by Sir Walter Raleigh to explore the Atlantic coast of America. They returned full of enthusiasm for the fertile soil and the delightful climate of Virginia. They praised also the kindness of the Indians, who provided them with the best of food—deer, hares, fish, walnuts, melons, cucumbers, peas, and corn.

CAPTAIN JOHN SMITH.

(From the history of Virginia, by Captain John Smith.)

Apparently there was an abundance of food in the New World—flesh, fish, fruits, nuts, vegetables, and grain. The sailors were not farmers, however; nor were the colonists who came over the next year. They had no knowledge of the labor necessary to till the soil and raise the food, and after a year on Roanoke Island they returned to England.

Twenty years later the colonists at Jamestown were no more ready to labor at farming than those at Roanoke had been. Numbers died from hunger during the first summer, but the leader, John Smith, was able, from his own strength of character, to hold survivors to the work until a fair abundance of corn had been obtained. Meanwhile Smith managed to buy or borrow provisions from the Indians.

The settlers at Plymouth arrived in early winter and found a climate much colder than that of England or Holland. They could not hope to harvest a crop before the next autumn, and they also were dependent upon the red men for many months.

Soon after the *Mayflower* arrived in Provincetown harbor an expedition was sent out to search for the best spot to build a village. They followed the tracks of Indians, but could not find them nor their dwellings. The first sign of human life was a piece of clear ground which had been planted some years before. Going a little farther they found a field in which the stubble was new, showing that the ground had been recently cultivated. Finally they came upon "heaps of sand newly paddled with their hands." Led by curiosity the Pilgrims digged in these places and found several baskets filled with corn. This grain seemed to the Pilgrims a "very goodly sight," though they had never seen corn before. They carried the grain back to the ship, and when the Indians who owned the corn were found, the Pilgrims gladly paid them its full value.

When spring came the colonists at Plymouth began making preparations for planting. An Indian, named Squanto, who had previously been carried to England and had learned to speak some English, showed himself very friendly. He taught them how to prepare the fish which must be put in every hill for a fertilizer. He directed the planting and cultivating of the fields. As a result they had "a good increase." They were not so successful in other ways, for their barley crop was very light and their peas dried up with the sun.

A curious story is found in some old records. The dogs in a Plymouth colony town caused the farmers great trouble by digging up the alewives which they were accustomed to place in the hills. Therefore a law was passed that required the owner of every dog either to keep him securely tied for forty days after the fields were prepared, or to tie a forepaw to his head so that it would be impossible for the dog to dig in the newly prepared hill.

Two years later the Pilgrims are said to have had nearly sixty acres of ground well planted with corn, and many gardens filled with fruits and vegetables. However, the crop was light, mainly because the colonists had been too weak, from lack of food, properly to attend to it. A famine would have followed for the third time had not a vessel arrived from England, in August, bringing provisions sufficient for the winter.

For several years the Pilgrims were compelled to live partly upon wild game and fish. One summer their main support was obtained by the use of the only boat that remained, with which they caught large quantities of bass. They also obtained clams when they could not get fish, used ground-nuts in place of bread, and caught many wild fowl in the creeks and marshes.

The colonists had no milk, butter, nor cheese for the first three years in Plymouth. There were no domestic animals in New England until, in the spring of 1623, a vessel arrived bringing the first cows. In time beef and veal were added to the list of foods, and soon other domestic animals were brought over. By the middle of the fourth summer the village of New Plymouth was reported to have nearly two hundred inhabitants, with some cattle and goats, and many swine and poultry.

The tools used by the early colonists were, like their houses and furniture, of the rudest manufacture. Agriculture, such as exists in the United States to-day, was entirely unknown two centuries ago. The plow was little used and the few plows among the colonists were inconvenient, heavy tools. The important planting and cultivating implement used by the farmers was the hoe.

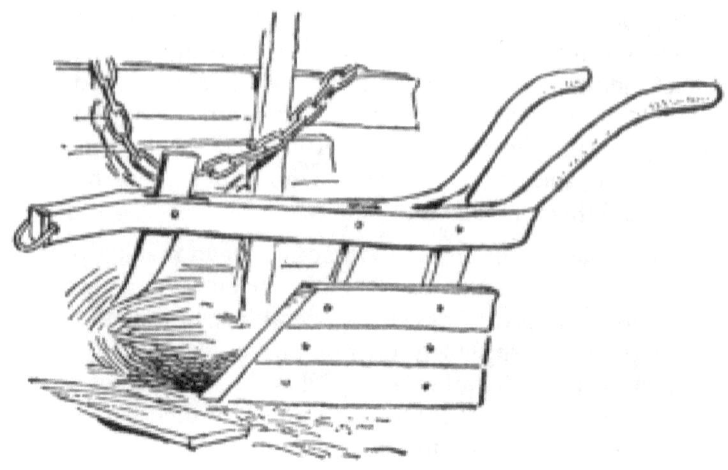

AN ANCIENT PLOW.

The village or plantation blacksmith made the tools for the farmers, and they were rudely formed and shaped. In harvest time the hoe was again called into use, as well as the roughly constructed scythes and pruninghooks. The muscle-developing flail separated the grain from the straw, and the miller ground it into meal, or flour, taking "toll" for his pay—that is, a fixed fraction of the product.

How the system of agriculture has changed during these two centuries, or rather during the last century, for few of the improvements are yet a hundred years old! As in the methods of producing heat and light, inventions have done wonders in providing us with a greater amount and a larger variety of food at a reduced cost. Formerly all farm-work was done by the use of great muscular power. Only a strong man can wield the hoe for hours at a time. To walk behind a plow, guiding the horse and holding the plow in place, is no light task. To swing a scythe from early morning until late in the day severely taxes the strength. To thresh grain upon the barn floor with a flail day after day needs much physical endurance. The labor of many men was required to manage even a comparatively small farm. To-day all these conditions are changed.

At the present time "the most desirable farm-hand is the man with the cunning brain who can get the most work out of a machine without breaking it. The farm laborer finds himself advanced to the ranks of skilled labor. The man who plows uses his muscle only in guiding the machine. The man who operates the harrow has half a dozen levers to lighten his labor. The sower walks leisurely behind a drill and works brakes. The reaper needs a quick brain and a quick hand—not necessarily a strong arm nor a powerful back. The threshers are merely assistants to a machine. The men who heave the wheat into the bins only press buttons."

CHAPTER III.

IMPLEMENTS FOR PLANTING.

George was determined to be a farmer. He was but twelve years of age, yet he felt sure that he knew his own mind. He said to himself and to his friends that life out of doors, life on a farm, was the best and healthiest kind of life. He declared that to raise the food of the world was the most important service that man could do for his fellow-beings.

The boy lived in a city. He had always lived in a city and had never seen a farm. He had never been away from home. His home was a flat, or apartment, occupying a portion of one floor of a ten-story block. His knowledge of life was limited entirely to city life. He had been to the park; he had seen there trees and shrubbery, grass and flowers. Yet he had never visited the park alone; he had never seen any of the work needed in caring for the trees and flowers. He knew absolutely nothing about gardening or farming; he could not tell the difference between a hoe and a rake; he would not be able to answer the simplest questions about farm life.

Yet George had decided to be a farmer, and he had made up his mind to study the subject of farming at once. He proposed to ask Uncle Ben all sorts of questions every chance he could get. He intended to obtain books from the library that would tell him what he needed to know. Oh, could he only go into the country, try for himself life upon a farm, and see with his own eyes what a farmer had to do!

So George went to work. He did not neglect his school duties, but carefully prepared his daily lessons. When these were done he was ready to study agriculture. He did not know where to begin with books, so he asked questions.

"Uncle Ben," he said one evening as the family was gathered around the library lamp, "how does it happen that a farmer sometimes raises tomatoes and sometimes potatoes? What does he do if he wants one rather than the other?"

"Well, George," was the laughing reply, "I think that you have much to learn before you make a successful farmer. Don't you know that if he wants potatoes he plants potatoes?"

"Why, I suppose so," said George. "Then if he desires apples, does he plant apples?"

"Hardly," said his uncle. "Seeds would be better than entire apples."

George was started and for the rest of the evening he asked no more questions, his whole attention being turned to the large encyclopedia on his knee. When next he plied his uncle with questions it was evident that he had already learned something.

"When a farmer plants a potato, he puts it in a hole and covers it up. I have read that he plows the ground first. What does he do that for?"

"For two reasons, I suppose," replied Uncle Ben. "The roots and sprouts grow better in a soil that has been softened. When the ground is unplowed, it is baked hard. Besides, plowing turns the soil over, brings new dirt to the top, and generally mixes it all together."

"Oh, yes!" said George. "Then I must learn about plowing first."

George obtained as good a knowledge of plows and tillage as was possible from books. In order fully to understand the subject, it would be necessary to see the plows and use them. But that could not come yet. The books told him that the earliest and simplest way to till the soil was with a spade. From them George learned, what most boys and girls know, what a spade was, and that a spade was all that was absolutely needed to soften the soil and prepare it for planting.

To spade a piece of ground is slow work; it is also hard work. Could not some method be devised so that the spading or tilling could be done by horses or oxen? This led to the invention of the plow. This was made thousands of years ago. The kooloo plow, still in use in India, was one of the earliest and was very rude. It was made entirely of wood, the sharp part of the plow being like a thorn in shape, but very thick and strong.

As the centuries went on, iron began to be used; and early in the history of iron it was applied to plows. They were still made of wood, but iron plates were placed over the wood, where the instrument tore into the ground. Later the plow itself was made of iron, leaving the handles still formed of wood. This iron plow would sometimes become covered with soil and so be almost useless. This was corrected by the use of steel shares instead of iron. This brought George to the modern plow.

George was not content with simply obtaining an idea about plows; he wished to know all that he could about them. He obtained books that gave complete accounts of the varieties of plows, the ways in which they were used, and the work which they should do. He learned that a plow should be fitted to its task. It should be as light as possible, easily drawn, and it should run with even steadiness, at a uniform depth. It should not only turn the soil over, but should thoroughly powder it and bury the weeds.

To his great surprise George also learned that some of the modern plows were as much superior to the ordinary plow as that was to the spade. The sulky plow is easier for the horses than the common plow; it makes furrows of different depths; and it has a seat for the farmer. Sometimes several plowshares are placed side by side and drawn by a large number of horses. This is called a gang plow. Steam and wind and water and even electricity are coming into use to furnish power for plows, in place of the animal power of horses.

"Well, Uncle Ben," said George one evening, "now I understand something about plowing and tillage. The next thing a farmer does in the spring is to plant his potatoes and corn, is it not?"

"Yes," was the reply.

"Well, then," said George, "that will not take me long to learn. All there is to do is to dig a hole, put in the potato, and cover it with earth."

"I am afraid that you will find that the job is not quite so simple as that. Has the farmer nothing to plant but potatoes?" asked the uncle.

"Yes," said the boy. "Corn and turnips and oats and wheat and pumpkins and lots of other things."

"Would you plant a kernel of corn in just the same way that you would a potato?"

"No, I suppose not," was the reply.

"And do you think that every farmer does all his planting by hand? Does he not have tools to help him?"

Thus George was started on a new line of thought. He read of the sower, as he slowly walks the length of the field, throwing the grain right and left. Even this work is better and more quickly done by machinery. The hand sower is a little machine which the farmer straps to his shoulders. The hopper of the sower is filled with grain and, as the handle is turned, the grain is scattered broadcast to as great a distance as possible. More saving of labor still is the horse sower, which is simply the hand sower on a larger scale. Sometimes the seed is inserted in the ground by means of grain drills, which deposit the grain more evenly and at the same time cover it with earth.

After learning how to sow seed, George began to inquire into the subject of planting. Many machines have been invented for this purpose which save much labor. The most important are the corn planter and the potato planter. Machines for planting other vegetables are much like these. The hand corn planter, which is used on small farms, is carried in the hand of the farmer. At each place where he wishes a hill of corn he strikes into the ground the planter, which leaves the kernels at the proper depth and covers them with soil. The horse corn planter is a form of grain drill, which does the same work as the hand planter.

The potato planter is a simple machine, though it does a variety of work. It cuts the potatoes into slices and drops them through a tube into a furrow which the plow-like part of the planter makes. The slices are dropped at regular spaces and are covered with dirt by the machine itself. In other words, the farmer puts potatoes in the hopper and drives the machine the length of the field. The planter does the rest of the work, saving the farmer the labor of slicing the potatoes, digging the hole, dropping the vegetable and covering it with earth.

All this and much more George learned during the next two weeks. Then he showed that he was ready for a new subject by asking his uncle what the farmer did between seedtime and harvest.

"I suppose," said the boy, "that most farmers get their planting done almost before summer begins. Then it must be some time before they begin to harvest the grain and dig the potatoes. What do they do all summer?"

"I think," replied his uncle, "that you will have to go into the country and see some things for yourself. As the school term is nearly finished, I believe that you must visit a good farmer and spend the summer and autumn with him. Then you will know something of a real farmer's life and work. But to answer your question by asking another, Did you ever hear of weeds?"

After that George asked few questions. He began to think that he was showing too much ignorance. From that evening until the end of June he had no thoughts but of the farm. He read but little and waited to study his subject at close hand. But he did discover that a farmer's life is not too easy in the summer. He learned that the ground must be kept free from weeds and continually loosened. He found that the farmer uses his hoe in deadly hostility to the weeds; that he makes his horse do a part of the work of hoeing; that the harrow and the cultivator keep the soil loose between the rows.

When the summer came, George felt that he had some knowledge of tillage, of sowing and planting, and of weeding; this was book knowledge. Now he hoped to get into the inside and learn something of the farmer's methods of harvesting. "Then," he thought, "I can be a farmer."

CHAPTER IV.

IMPLEMENTS FOR HARVESTING.

GEORGE awoke the first morning at the farm to hear the roosters crowing, the cows mooing, the sheep bleating, and the men cheerily whistling as they hurried about the chores. No thought of turning over for another nap entered his head, but in quick time he was dressed and ready for the morning meal. Breakfast over, George hastened out of doors and was soon eagerly watching Tom, who had been directed to cut the grass around the edges of one of the fields which had been previously mowed. Here for the first time he saw a scythe and learned its use.

For a while George watched Tom's steady swing of the scythe as he slowly cut a swath the length of the field. Then he hastened to another field where the mowing machine was steadily moving across the lot. What an improvement! What a saving of labor! How easily those knives moved through the grass, laying every spire low as soon as it was touched! How much more even the cut, though Tom was skilled with the scythe! The horses drew the machine with ease and the driver had a comfortable seat. However, it was plain that he must keep his head clear and his eyes open, to properly attend to every part of the instrument.

MOWING WITH SCYTHES.

When noon came George was tired and heated, and he gladly remained in the house after dinner. Here he found his favorite encyclopedia and was soon hunting up the history of the invention of the mower. He was surprised to learn how short a time it had been in use. From the beginning of history the crooked sickle and the straighter scythe had been almost the only tools used for cutting grass and grain. Not until about the middle of the present century had practical mowing machines come into use. But now, except on very small or rocky farms, the horse mower is an absolute necessity.

The next day George again visited the fields to see the next step in the process of making hay. First he found Tom, with a fork, turning over the grass which he had mowed the day before. Then he went to the other field, where he saw the same work being done by a machine. The mower had left the grass in heaps so that the sun could reach only the surface. It is necessary that hay should be thoroughly dried as quickly as possible. Across the field and back again went the hay tedder, its forks picking up the grass and tossing it in every direction. One horse only was needed, and the driver was a boy.

The third day George was again in the field. Once more the grass was turned. Then in the late afternoon it was prepared for the barn. Tom could only use the small hand rake, for his work was close to the fence; he was simply cleaning up what the machines had failed to reach. But in the field where George had watched the mower and the tedder, machinery and horse power were again in use. A horse went back and forth, drawing a horse rake behind him. Now and then, at regular intervals, up came the rake, a pile of hay was left, and on went the horse. Then a hay sweep passed along at right angles to the rake and soon the hay was in piles. As the field was very smooth and free from stones, a hay loader was used to place the hay upon the wagon. A boy drove the horses, two men laid the load, and soon the wagon was started for the barn. The old-fashioned, slow, hard work of lifting the hay by the forkful into the barn was no longer necessary. Hay forks, run by horse power, grappled the hay, and lifted the load. Conveyers carried the hay to the right point and dropped it in the mow.

Such was the work done during the first three days that George spent on the farm. He saw the old-fashioned hand work and the modern use of labor-saving machinery. Then he studied his books. In them he found that the hand labor of cutting, drying, and housing the hay used to cost about five dollars a ton, and that now, with the best of modern machines, it need cost not more than one dollar a ton. This machinery is of great value to the farmer and also to those who buy the hay; for the farmer can sell his hay at a lower price, since it costs him less to make it.

This was the last of the haying. For several weeks George watched the hoes and the harrows, as they kept the gardens and fields in good condition. Then came harvest-time. Potatoes were first in George's thoughts, and when he learned that they were to be dug on the morrow he was thoroughly aroused. But he met with a sore disappointment. The potatoes were not dug by machinery. The common hoe or the specially shaped potato hoe were the only tools. Then the back-aching work of picking up potatoes added to his disgust, and he declared that he never would raise many potatoes. He learned that plows sometimes help the hoes, but that potato-digging machines have never come into general use, though good ones have been invented.

At last grain harvest-time came. This was the time to which George had long looked forward. Now he could see the wheat cut and threshed. This he was sure was the best work of the farmer. But when he saw Tom take the short, crooked sickle, cut some grain with that, gather it in his arms, and tie a cord around it, he could scarcely control himself. "Is that the way grain is harvested?" he said. Then when he saw the grain laid on the barn floor and struck rapidly by flails in the hands of two men, he declared, "If that is what the farmer has to do to get a little grain, then I do not want to be a farmer."

"Well," said Mr. Miller, "that is just what all farmers had to do until within fifty years."

A REAPER AND BINDER.

But George soon saw a different method. This first hand-work had been merely to harvest a small amount of early grain; a few days later the machines were brought out. Now George was happy. At last he saw a reaping machine and a combined reaper and binder. This interested him the most. He watched the machine as the horses drew it along the edge of the standing grain. He saw the grain cut and laid upon a platform, carried up into the machine, taken by two arms called packers, gathered by them into bundles, bound by cords and thrown to the ground. What more could be asked of any machine?

And yet there is a new type of harvester that has been used in San Joaquin valley, California. It cuts a swarth fifty-two feet in width. It not only cuts the grain but it threshes it as well. It makes the sacks and fills them as it travels over the field. It is said to cut an area of a hundred acres a day, and at the same time thresh the grain and fill fifteen hundred sacks.

THE MCCORMICK REAPER.

Later in the autumn came the thresher. That belonging to Farmer Miller was run by horse power. Two horses stood upon a platform, constantly stepping forward but not moving from their position. Instead the platform moved backward and this turned the machinery. The men placed the grain stalks in the hopper and the threshed grain came out of the machine, flowing into sacks, which when filled were tied by the men and set aside ready for the market.

The reaper and the thresher seemed to George the greatest of inventions. He obtained a book on inventions, and for many days he was buried in it. He read of the Englishman, Henry Ogle, whose reaper, made in 1822, aroused the anger of the working people, who threatened to kill the manufacturers if they continued to make the machines; of Patrick Bell's invention, which, though successful, was forgotten for twenty or thirty years; of Cyrus H. McCormick, the American, whose reaper first obtained a lasting success.

Most of all he was interested in the account of the first trial of reapers in England, at the time of the world's fair in 1851. What a joke it was for the London *Times* to poke fun at the McCormick machine, as it was exhibited in the Crystal Palace! How the great newspaper did wish that it had kept quiet when a few days later it was compelled to report the complete success of the ridiculed reaper!

The trial took place in Essex, about forty-five miles from London. Two hundred farmers were present, ready to laugh at failure or to accept any successful machine. The wheat was not ripe; the crop was heavy; and the day was rainy. The Hussey reaper was first tried but was soon clogged by the green, wet grain. The judges proposed to discontinue the trial, as the conditions were so unfavorable. But the agent of the McCormick reaper protested. His machine would work under any conditions; he wished that the gentlemen who had taken the pains to come to the trial should have a chance to see the McCormick. Accordingly it was brought forward and, in spite of everything, it went steadily forward, cutting all before it. Success was evident, and the English farmers gave three hearty cheers for the American reaping-machine.

Another trial, at which the reaper was timed, showed that it could cut twenty acres a day with ease. Even the laboring men realized that the machine would come at once into use; one, who was among the interested spectators, took the sickle, which he happened to have with him, and broke it in two across his knee; he said that he would no longer need that.

Four years later a trial took place in France also. Here three American, two English, and two French machines were tested. McCormick's reaper easily came out ahead, with the other American machines close behind. At the same time four threshing machines were tested. Six men with their flails, working as hard as they could, obtained fifty-four quarts of wheat in half an hour; the American thresher gave out six hundred and seventy-three quarts in the same time!

THRESHING WITH FLAIL.

We have spent much time on farming machinery. We must now leave George to a further study of farm life and farm work. So far he has only examined tools and machinery. He has learned from experience, however, that a modern farmer has much more than this to learn, and much work to do that cannot be done by machinery. He realizes that much study is needed to make a successful farmer. He finds that nearly every State in the Union has one or more agricultural colleges, and that the United States does its share in giving aid and information to farmers. He still desires to be a farmer, but he is glad that it is a modern farmer that he must be. He goes back to school, eager to prepare himself to enter the best agricultural college that he can find, in order that he may be ready for intelligent farming as soon as opportunity comes.

CHAPTER V.

SOIL.

A LITTLE boat was sailing along the north shore of Massachusetts bay. It was a shallop belonging to the fishing hamlet of Cape Ann. In it were Gov. Roger Conant and a few of his friends. After a sail of a dozen miles the boat was turned to the westward and entered a harbor. On it went until it reached a point of land which separated two little rivers. Upon this peninsula, which the Indians called Naumkeag, Conant landed. He walked across from one stream to the other; he carefully examined the trees, the weeds, the grass, and the remains of an Indian cornfield. Then he sailed back to the cape.

COLONISTS IN A SHALLOP.

A few weeks later Governor Conant and fourteen companions moved from Cape Ann to Naumkeag, now Salem. For three years the hamlet on the cape had been struggling for life. The colonists had at last become disheartened and had abandoned the settlement. But what better fortune could they expect at Naumkeag? Conant's study of the little peninsula had taught him that here was a fertile soil from which he could raise food enough for the colonists. Cape Ann had not proved fertile. It was a "stern and rock-bound coast." The entire cape seemed to be one vast ledge of granite rock, and only here and there could grain and vegetables be grown.

The settlement of Salem was four years earlier than that of Boston, and but six years after the Pilgrims arrived in Plymouth. Thus early in the history of the colonies was it found necessary to seek fertile soils for settlements. As these grew and the number of the colonists increased, the need of more land and better soil became apparent. Ten years after Conant went to Naumkeag, the population of three entire towns near Boston moved, through woods, over hills and valleys, and across streams, to the fertile valley of the Connecticut River. Farms spread out in every direction until, before the middle of the eighteenth century, nearly all of southern New England was dotted with them.

The French and Indian War came, and at its close the valley of the Ohio River was placed in the hands of the English. Then followed the American Revolution, and the Northwest Territory became a part of the United States. The New England farmers had become crowded by this time, and many were eager for more land. A new migration followed. Farmers from New England, New York, and Pennsylvania began to journey westward and to settle the Northwest Territory. Ohio soon had sufficient population to be made a State. Indiana and Illinois followed, then Michigan and Wisconsin. Meanwhile the United States purchased the great province of Louisiana, and Iowa, Minnesota, and Nebraska were settled by the Eastern farmers and others who had come across the ocean from Europe.

Never in the history of the world had there been such a rapid settlement of new lands. It has continued even up to the present time. A few years ago the new territory of Oklahoma was opened to farmers, and its growth has been remarkable.

The principal reason for this rapid settlement of Western land may be found in the excellent character of the soil. For ages it had lain uncultivated, waiting for the coming of the white man. Unlike the rocky portions of New England, the ground seldom contains a large stone. Unlike the hills and valleys of the coast States, the interior territory is prairie land, level as far as the eye can see. Here the gang plows can be run; here the mowing machines and the mammoth harvesters can be used to great advantage.

Thus grew the northern part of the United States. In the South the westward movement was not so rapid. The conditions of agriculture were different. The climate of South Carolina was unlike that of Massachusetts; the cold of New York was unknown in Georgia. In New England small farms were the rule; on these the work was done by the owner, with the aid of his sons or perhaps a hired man or two. In Virginia large plantations were common; here the proprietor lived at his ease and the land was cultivated by slaves. In Connecticut the crops raised were used for the most part by the farmer's family or sold in the immediate neighborhood. In North Carolina the products of the plantations were exported in great quantities.

In time, however, these Southern people became dissatisfied with their early territory, as their Northern brothers had been, and gradually new States were formed to the westward. Kentucky and Tennessee were followed by Louisiana; Alabama and Mississippi were formed on one side of the great river, but a few years before Missouri and Arkansas were on the other. State after State was admitted to the Union as soon as a sufficient number of people had flocked into them, and the number of Territories was steadily diminishing.

At the farther end of the continent, the Oregon country, saved to us by the heroism of Dr. Marcus Whitman, added a large territory of extremely fertile soil. South of Oregon the great State of California was added to the Union, as a result of Marshall's discovery of gold at Sutter's Fort. Yet California to-day is a State for the farmer as well as the miner. Thus finally, the Atlantic coast, the region of the Great Lakes, the Ohio valley, the Gulf States, the valley of the "Father of Waters," and the Pacific slope—in fact, almost all sections of the United States—were well peopled by farmers, drawing from the rich virgin soil immense crops of food, more than sufficient for our own people.

AN IRRIGATING TRENCH.

But we were not satisfied. In the very heart of the country, between Kansas,

Nebraska, and the Dakotas on the east, and California, Oregon, and Washington on the west, lay a great region which had no attractions for the farmer. Let him properly plow and cultivate the soil, let him add to it soil-food or fertilizers as much as he pleases, let the spring and the summer come, and let the hot sun add its part to change the seed into growing grain—in spite of all the farmer's efforts no crop could be obtained. The grain dried up almost as soon as planted. There was no water. For month after month no rain fell upon this region. It was called the "Great American Desert."

The first attempt to make this desert soil yield a suitable return for the labor of the farmer was made at Salt Lake City. Fifty years ago a band of earnest men braved cold and famine, and the even more deadly Indians, crossed the great region west of the Mississippi River, and made a settlement in the very midst of the desert country. To-day the desert of Utah blooms like a garden; the soil is fertile and yields large returns to the industrious inhabitants. What has made the change? Nothing but water.

If the heavens refuse to send rain to moisten the parched ground, cannot the needed water be obtained in some other way? The pioneer settlers of Salt Lake led the way in teaching mankind that the ground may be irrigated by human means. Water may be carried to the fields where, flowing along the surface of the ground, it soaks in until it reaches the roots of the crops. The water may be pumped out of the ground or it may be brought from the mountains in trenches or pipes. This method of helping nature by providing water where rain is scarce is called irrigation.

In the same way many other sections of the great West have been reclaimed. Southern California, formerly fit only for the raising of vast herds of cattle, is now the great orchard of the country. Large portions of New Mexico and Arizona now add to the general stock of food. Irrigation bids fair to be of vast benefit to the country as, little by little, barren lands are rendered fertile.

At present the principal grain region of our country is the great Northwest, the twelve States west of Pennsylvania. The principal grain is corn, and two-thirds of the entire crop of this country is grown in the seven States of Ohio, Indiana, Illinois, Iowa, Nebraska, Kansas, and Missouri. The banner corn State is Iowa.

The wheat crop is more valuable to the world than the corn. The United States raises one-quarter of all the wheat grown in the world, and the great Northwest produces two-thirds of that. Wheat can be profitably raised in a cooler climate than is suitable for corn; therefore the five Northern States Michigan, Wisconsin, Minnesota, North and South Dakota add their quota to the wheat grown in the seven great corn States. Minnesota leads in the production of wheat. Not all the wheat comes from this region, however, for two Pacific States, California and Oregon, produce one-eighth of the entire crop of our country, and Pennsylvania gives a large share.

Iowa leads in the production of oats as well as of corn; more than two-thirds of the oat crop comes from the Northwest. New York and Pennsylvania add their quota, about one-eighth of the total crop. The Northwest thus provides two-thirds of the grain, on much less than one-half of the cultivated land of the United States.

A RICE FIELD.

Though grain is the great agricultural product, it is not the only crop that we raise in large quantities. Ten of the Southern States furnish each year more than sixty thousand tons of rice, a large portion of which comes from Louisiana and South Carolina.

The United States is just beginning to take rank as a sugar-producing country. We now raise about one-eighth of the sugar that we use each year. At present most of the sugar comes from sugar cane, which is grown mainly in Louisiana; but the central States and California have recently begun the manufacture of sugar from beets, and beet-growing is becoming an important industry. The recent annexation of islands in the West Indies and the Pacific Ocean greatly increases our sugar production.

Two other crops which are obtained from the soil must not be forgotten, although they are neither of them foods. The Gulf States furnish nine-elevenths of all the cotton raised in the world, and the States north of them produce a large portion of the world's tobacco. Kentucky leads in the production of the latter staple, raising each year nearly one-half of the tobacco grown in the United States.

Grain, cotton, tobacco, rice, and sugar are the main products of the soil in the United States. Each of these is produced in its own special region, depending upon the character of the soil and the climate. The value of our agricultural exports is rapidly increasing, and the world is looking more and more to the United States to furnish a large part of the food necessary for all mankind.

CHAPTER VI.

A MODERN DINNER.

GEORGE BAXTER and his wife returned to New York, after a winter spent in California just a week before Mrs. Baxter's sister and her husband were preparing to start for a second summer in Europe. A third sister, Alice Smith, decided to give the travelers a small dinner, to which only the family should be invited.

A DINNER PARTY.

When the evening arrived, eleven members of the Atwood family gathered about the table in Mr. Smith's capacious dining room, the seat of honor being given to the mother, Mrs. Atwood. Besides the three married couples, Frank and Alice Smith, Albert and Mary Fremont, and George and Lucy Baxter, there were the four unmarried children. James, the oldest son, was a banker in the city; Walter, next younger than Lucy, was a student fitting for Columbia University; Fred and Mabel were still classed as school children.

After the trim waiter had brought on the soup, the moment's quiet was broken by George Baxter, who said to the hostess: "How good to get back to New York once more, if only to get a soup that one can eat without burning the mouth with the sharp condiments. You have no seasoning at all in the soup, have you, Alice?"

"Oh, yes," replied the hostess," it is a very simple soup, but there is the usual pepper and salt. What have you been in the habit of having?"

"I am sure that I could tell what we did not have in some of our Mexican soups much easier than what we did have. I should think that there must have been both kinds of pepper, ginger, garlic, mustard, horseradish, Worcestershire sauce, and everything else. I cannot understand why people living in the tropics want to season their food with such hot stuff."

"What do you mean by two kinds of pepper, brother George?" asked Mabel.

"Cayenne pepper and black pepper," was the reply.

"Oh, yes, I know!" said Fred. "Cayenne pepper comes from Cayenne in French Guiana. But where do we get black pepper?"

"Nearly all of it comes from Sumatra," said Mary. "Do you know where Sumatra is, Mabel?"

"Sumatra is one of the large islands south and southeast of Asia, which are called the East Indies," replied the schoolgirl.

The conversation had now become general, and Mr. Smith called attention to the distance that these condiments travel in reaching us.

"Sumatra is almost exactly on the opposite side of the earth from us," said he. "Fred, how would the black pepper be brought to New York from Sumatra?"

"Across the Indian Ocean and the Red Sea, through the Suez Canal and the Mediterranean Sea, I suppose. But I do not know whether it would then come straight across the Atlantic Ocean, or first go to England."

"Usually," said Mr. Smith," it would go to England first."

"Alice," broke in Mabel," what else is in the soup beside pepper? Oh, I know, salt. Is salt also brought half-way round the world?"

"I know where salt comes from," said Fred;" up State. It is dug out of the ground near Syracuse."

"That is right, Fred," said James. "But New York State does not supply all the salt used in this country. For years many ships and barks have come yearly into Gloucester harbor from Sicily, bringing salt for the fishing-schooners. Steamers even are being used to bring salt from the Mediterranean Sea, in order that the Gloucester fishermen may send salt fish all over our country."

"We must not forget," said Mrs. Smith, "that there is rice in our soup also. That comes from South Carolina."

Just then the plates were removed and the fish was brought on.

"This is a rarity," said the hostess. "Can you tell us what it is, James?"

"I think so. It is halibut, is it not?"

"Why do you call it a rarity?" asked Mary.

"This halibut came from the Grand Banks," said Mrs. Smith. "I do not understand how they get it here so fresh."

James, who seemed to be quite familiar with the Gloucester fisheries, said: "The fishermen brought their load of halibut to the Gloucester wharves last night and immediately loaded it upon the Boston steamer. Three o'clock in the morning was its time for sailing, and at six it was being unloaded in Boston. The six-hour trains brought some of it to New York in time for our dinner."

LOADING FISH AT GLOUCESTER.

"Steamers and railroad trains seem necessary for our dinner, do they not?" said Albert. "But this fish sauce contains only articles from nearer home, I am sure."

"Do not be too certain of that," said Mr. Smith. "Alice, what is there in this sauce?"

"First, there are eggs."

"Those came from our Long Island farm, of course," said her husband.

"Then there is olive oil."

"That comes from Italy," said Mr. Smith. "That is not a home product. The olives that you are eating are, of course, from Italy also."

"I doubt that," said George. "I was just about to remark that these olives had come from California. I can easily detect the taste."

"Yes, "the hostess added. "These olives I bought just to see if George and Lucy would notice that they were not our usual queen olives. They are said to have come from Pomona."

"That is a great olive center," said George.

"What else is there in the sauce, Alice?" asked her husband.

"Pepper and salt, vinegar— —"

"Cider vinegar, I suppose," broke in Mrs. Baxter. "How much nicer apple vinegar is than grape vinegar! Most of the vinegar that we had in California was made from wine. That State is becoming a great grape-producing region. But do you know, Frank, where the apples were grown?"

"No," said Mr. Smith, "but probably they were raised either in Vermont or New Hampshire. Last year the New York apple orchards gave but a poor yield, while those of New England did much better. Probably this season will prove an off year for Vermont apples, but we shall have all that we can use in our own State."

"A little lemon ends the list," said the hostess.

"Lemons from Sicily, I suppose," remarked Mr. Baxter. "Have you tried the California lemons yet?"

"Yes," said Mr. Smith. "We can sometimes get very fine lemons from California, but not always. If the growers of lemons were more particular about the quality of the fruit that they send out, there would be a better trade in California lemons."

While this conversation was going on, the fish was removed and a roast of beef was placed on the table, and with it the vegetables. The different members of the family had become quite interested in the discussion by this time, and it was continued as a matter of course.

"This is a good piece of beef," remarked James Atwood. "What are we going to do for meat when the natural increase in the amount of land devoted to cultivation uses up all the grazing regions?"

"You need not fret about that," said Mr. Baxter; "that will not come in your day. You ought to take a trip through Texas, New Mexico, and Arizona, through Wyoming and Montana, or other sections of the Rocky Mountain region, and you would not fear for our cattle-raising interests."

"Here, again, the railroads are important," said Mr. Fremont. "What numbers of long freight trains daily come east, loaded with cattle for New York and Boston, and even for Great Britain and the Continent. The European consumption of our cattle is of great and rapidly growing importance."

A CATTLE TRAIN.

"These new potatoes came from the Bermudas," remarked the host.

"And the peas from Maryland," added the hostess. "Do you not think that these are remarkably fresh after having been brought so far?"

"How about the lettuce?" asked James. "That must have come from some greenhouse."

"Without doubt, though I did not inquire," replied Mrs. Smith.

Not willing to leave anything out of the conversation, Mabel here inquired about the macaroni and tomatoes.

"The macaroni comes from Italy," replied her sister Mary. "Much of it is shipped from Genoa, the city which claims to have been the birthplace of Columbus. You would find it interesting, Mabel, to read about the production and preparation of macaroni."

"The tomatoes were canned on our farm last autumn," said Mrs. Smith. "We think them much superior to any that we can buy."

After this the conversation turned upon the bread. There were two kinds, white and brown. One of the ladies remarked that she never ate white bread; bread from whole wheat flour was so much more wholesome. Another said that graham bread was good enough for her. They talked about the white flour, made in Minneapolis, from Dakota wheat. They spoke of the Indian meal made from corn grown in Iowa. They wondered why so little rye was used in this country, since it is the staple grain in Russia. They then inquired concerning the other substances used in making the two kinds of bread.

"Where does the butter come from?" asked Mrs. Fremont.

"This particular box is marked from Delaware County, New York," replied the hostess. "Most of the creameries that send butter to New York City are located at some distance from the railroads. The farms nearer the railroads send all their milk to the city. But the farmers that are too remote profitably to send in the milk make the cream into butter and cheese. They then feed the buttermilk to the pigs."

"That is a new thought to me," said James. "So it seems that some products are made only where there are no railroads."

"Or where there is no great city within a few hundred miles," added Walter.

"I suppose there is molasses in this brown bread," said Lucy Baxter.

"Molasses comes from Porto Rico," said Mabel, who was studying the West Indies just at this time in her geography lessons at school.

"Some of it," said her oldest sister. "But most of the sugar comes from Cuba."

"But not all," said James. "This sugar has been traveling for nearly two weeks to reach New York. First a sea voyage of more than two thousand miles, and then a railroad journey of more than three thousand miles, and yet the section where it grew is a part of the United States."

"It must have come from Honolulu then," said Walter. "I wonder whether the Sandwich Islands, being now a part of the United States, will interfere with the raising of sugar cane in our Southern States?"

"Very little probably, but now that the United States possesses Hawaii and Porto Rico, it will scarcely be necessary for us to import any sugar and molasses," said Fred.

When the dessert and fruit were brought on, new subjects for conversation were found.

"What do you call this pudding, Alice?" asked her husband.

"It is a peach-tapioca pudding," was the reply. "The peaches are from Delaware; canned, of course."

"Here, again, the West Indies are represented," said James; "the tapioca came from Hayti."

"And the East Indies also," added Walter, "for I taste nutmeg, which comes from the Molucca Islands. These islands furnish such an amount of spice that they are commonly called the Spice Islands."

The discussion of foods continued throughout the dinner. The oranges, almost the last of the season, had been brought from California. Florida oranges were scarce that year. The bananas were from Mexico and almost a luxury. The war with Spain had destroyed trade with Cuba, from which island the great bulk of bananas had usually come.

Among the nuts were almonds that had been imported from Italy, filberts that had been sent across the ocean from England, and walnuts that had come from California. Finally the coffee was from the island of Java.

DRYING COFFEE IN JAVA.

Before the dinner party broke up, Mr. Smith reviewed the facts which had been learned in the conversation. He especially called attention to the small number of articles that are not profitably raised in the United States.

"We should miss our coffee very much," he said, "if our country were blockaded at any time. The loss of the banana would be the loss of a luxury. Had we no macaroni or tapioca we should still have enough to eat. Perhaps our taste would become more natural were we deprived of pepper. No other of the foods on this table should we be entirely deprived of, even were we separated wholly from the rest of the world. California could furnish us with olives, lemons, and almonds, as well as Italy does. We need not go to England for filberts, and even if we had not of late obtained new colonies, we could produce in time all the sugar we needed to supply the entire country. No other nation in the world is so well prepared to furnish its own food."

ELI WHITNEY.

A QUILTING BEE IN THE OLDEN TIME.

SECTION IV.
CLOTHING.

CHAPTER I.

COLONIAL CONDITIONS.

You all know that the United States of America was formed out of thirteen English colonies scattered along the Atlantic coast. Virginia was the first of these colonies to be founded, dating from 1607. Massachusetts was settled in 1620, New York in 1623, and so on until the last of the thirteen, Georgia, was established in 1733. From the time of these settlements until the Declaration of Independence in 1776, these colonies were subject to Great Britain and under her rule and control. The independence of these American colonies was a great loss to the British government, but it created a new nation of the same race which, together with the mother country, to-day holds the destiny of the world in its hands.

Great Britain for centuries has been largely a manufacturing country. It was the policy of the British government to control so far as possible manufactures and commerce for all her provinces and colonies. Hence during our colonial period the home government took every possible measure to prevent the introduction of manufactures into the colonies. We were dependent upon the mother country for cotton and woolen goods, cutlery, iron ware, and, indeed, almost everything that could be profitably manufactured in England and shipped to this country. Even after we had secured out independence, the strictest care was taken by the officials of England that drawings and models of machinery should not be brought to America.

As late as 1816 an American manufacturer of cotton cloth visited England. Although he carried letters of introduction which caused him to be treated with great courtesy and attention, he was refused permission to enter any of the cotton mills. The manufacturers suspected his purpose, which was to learn the construction of the "double speeder." Nevertheless he persisted, and one day, without permission and in spite of the sign "Positively no Admittance," he entered the carding-room, accompanied by a skilled mechanic. They proceeded as rapidly as possible to examine the machine, which was in full operation, but were soon ordered out by the overseer. They had, however, seen enough of its construction to enable them to make one.

After their return to this country they made a machine and set it up in the gentleman's cotton mill in the State of New York. The news of its successful operation reached England and aroused a jealous feeling among manufacturers. In their anger they planned a wicked scheme to destroy the life of the American manufacturer. A box containing an "infernal machine" was sent as freight on a packet ship bound for New York. Fortunately, when the crew was discharging the cargo, the box slipped from the car hook and fell with a crash upon the wharf. This caused it to explode, but without injury to any one.

In colonial times the condition of society was such as to make it almost impossible for the people to engage to any great extent in manufactures. The country was new and the principal business must be agriculture. After comfortable shelter for the families had been provided, every exertion must be put forth to secure food. Cloth could only be obtained from the mother country. Cotton and linen cloth were imported for shirts and sheets, woolen goods for clothing, a few silks for wedding dresses now and then, and leather for the shoes of all the people.

TAILOR AND COBBLER.

In the early times the tailor, with his goose and his shears, plied his trade from house to house, staying with each family long enough to make up the clothes necessary for the season. In like manner the shoemaker traveled about the country, with his kit upon his back, stopping with each household to make the shoes needed for the father, mother, and children.

These were the pioneer days, but, before we became a nation, the houses of the people had greatly improved in style of architecture and in comfort. Considerable wealth had been secured by many, and but little poverty was found anywhere. The mechanic arts were beginning to improve, and manufacturing, after a long and tedious waiting, was gradually making progress. At an early date sawmills had been established upon the streams, using the water as motive power. Gristmills had sprung up for grinding the grain raised by every farmer. The spinning wheel and the hand loom had found their place slowly but steadily in all parts of the country.

It is difficult to comprehend the great differences between the industries of those early days and the methods of doing business among us to-day. Now almost everything seems to be done by machinery, and the division of labor has been carried to such an extent that each laborer seems only an assistant to a machine. "You press the button, the machine does the rest."

FLAX WHEEL.

In the early days of our country, it was customary for the different members of a family to do almost everything that the necessities or comfort of the household required. Everywhere the farmer raised sheep, sheared them, carded the wool, spun it and wove it, all this being done upon the home farm. A well-to-do farmer would produce all the woolen cloth needed for clothing for himself and his family.

The sheep grazed upon the hills and their wool was clipped in the spring of the year. This wool was scoured, carded, spun by the family in the farmhouse, and then woven into cloth for the winter's wear. All this was done within the walls of the house, and the cloth was made up into clothing for the different members of the family by the itinerant tailor. What a contrast from the present system, which raises wool upon our Western hills and prairies, makes it into cloth in the large factories, and fashions it into trousers, vests, and coats in the great wholesale clothing establishments.

In some sections of the country the farmers raised flax, and from it made the purest white linen cloth. The writer of this chapter has in his possession a beautiful piece of white linen, woven upon the farm where he was born, from thread which was spun from flax raised upon the same farm. The flax wheel and the loom were also made by the father of the family.

If you could look into that old kitchen what a sight you would see! How quaint it would appear to each one of you! The kitchen makes an ell to the main house. This ell was an old house, built more than a century and a half ago, and moved up to the new house for a kitchen. In one corner stands the large spinning wheel; near it is the smaller flax wheel; in another corner stands the great wooden loom with its huge beam for the warp and its shuttle which must be thrown back and forth by hand. No carpet, not even an oil-cloth, is upon the floor, which is covered with pure white sand.

AN OLD-FASHIONED LOOM.

It would seem very strange to us if we were obliged to live surrounded by these primitive conditions. How much stranger would it appear to those who lived at that day if they could witness the improvements of our time!

CHAPTER II.

THE COTTON GIN.

In the quiet times that followed the French and Indian War, two years after the Treaty of 1763, Eli Whitney was born in Worcester County in Massachusetts. During the Revolutionary War he was busy making nails by hand, the only way in which nails were made in those days. He earned money enough by this industry and by teaching school to pay his way through college. But it was a slow process, and he was nearly twenty-seven years of age when he was graduated at Yale. Immediately upon his graduation he went to Georgia, — a long distance from home in those days, — having made an engagement to become a private tutor in a wealthy family of that State. On his arrival he found that the man who had engaged his services, unmindful of the contract, had filled the position with another tutor.

The widow of the famous Gen. Nathaniel Greene had a beautiful home at Mulberry Grove, on the Savannah River. Mrs. Greene invited young Whitney to make her house his home while he studied law. She soon perceived that he had great inventive genius. He devised several articles of convenience which Mrs. Greene much appreciated.

At that time the entire cotton crop of this country might have been produced upon a single field of two hundred acres. Cotton then commanded a very high price, because of the labor of separating the cotton fibre from the seed. The cotton clung to the seed with such tenacity that one man could separate the seed from only four or five pounds of cotton in a day. At that rate it would take him three months to make up a bale of clear cotton. Already inventions in machinery for the making of cotton cloth had made the production of cotton a necessity. Some means must be provided for a more rapid separation of cotton from the seed in order to make manufacturing profitable.

One day, one of Mrs. Greene's friends was regretting, in conversation with her, that there could be no profit in the cultivation of cotton. Mrs. Greene had great faith in the inventive powers of young Whitney, and she suggested that he be asked to make a machine which would separate the seed skillfully and rapidly, "for," said she, "Eli Whitney can make anything."

When the workmen in the deep mines of England needed a safety lamp to shield them from the explosions of the damp, they applied to the great chemist, Sir Humphrey Davy, and he invented one. So, these cotton raisers appealed to Mr. Whitney to invent for them a cotton engine or "gin." He knew nothing about either raw cotton or cotton seed. Could he be expected to invent a machine that would separate the cotton seed which he had never seen from the raw cotton which also he had never seen? But Whitney was an inventor. Trifles must not stand in his way. He secured samples of the cotton and the seed; even this was not an easy thing to do, for it was not the right season of the year.

A COTTON FIELD.

He began to work out his idea of the cotton gin, but met with many obstacles. There were no wire manufactories in the South and he could not obtain wire even in Savannah. Therefore he had to make his wire himself. Still further, he was obliged to manufacture his own iron tools. Step by step he overcame all obstacles, until he had a machine that he thought would answer the purpose.

A COTTON BALL.

Accordingly, one day, he entered the room where Mrs. Greene was conversing with friends and exclaimed, "The victory is mine!" All the guests, as well as the hostess, went with the inventor to examine the machine. He set the model in motion. It consisted of a cylinder four feet in length and five inches in diameter. Upon this was a series of circular saws half an inch apart and projecting two inches above the surface of the revolving cylinder. The saws passed through narrow slits between bars; these bars might be called the ribs of the hopper.

At once the saw teeth caught the cotton which had been placed in the hopper and carried it over between the bars. The seed was left behind, as it was too large to pass through. The saws revolved smoothly and the cotton was thoroughly separated from the seed. But after a few minutes the saws became clogged with the cotton and the wheels stopped. Poor Whitney was in despair. Victory was not yet his.

Mrs. Greene came to the rescue. Her housewifely instincts saw the difficulty at once and the remedy as well. "Here's what you want!" she exclaimed. She took a clothes brush hanging near by and held it firmly against the teeth of the saws. The cylinder began again to revolve, for the saws were quickly cleaned of the lint, which no longer clogged the teeth. "Madam," said the grateful Whitney, "you have perfected my invention."

The inventor added a second, larger cylinder, near the first. On this he placed a set of stiff brushes. As the two cylinders revolved, the brushes freed the saw teeth from the cotton and left it in the receiving pan.

THE COTTON GIN.

Thus the cotton gin was invented by the Yankee schoolmaster, Eli Whitney. Though improved in its workmanship and construction, it is still in use wherever cotton is raised. One man with a Whitney cotton gin can clean a thousand pounds of cotton in place of the five pounds formerly cleaned by hand.

When a safety lamp was needed, Davy invented it. When faster water travel was demanded, Fulton constructed the steamboat. When the world needed vast wheat fields, McCormick devised his reaper. When the time had come for the telegraph, Morse studied it out. In the fullness of time, Bell, Edison, and others invented the telephone. When a cotton gin was needed, Eli Whitney made it. Here again the law holds that "necessity is the mother of invention."

When a great invention is made, everybody wants the benefit of it, and people seem to think that the inventor "has no rights which they are bound to respect." Whitney secured a patent upon his machine, but, unmindful of that, a great many persons began to make cotton gins. He was immediately involved in numerous legal contests. Before he secured a single verdict in his favor he had sixty lawsuits pending. After many delays he finally secured the payment of $50,000 which the Legislature of South Carolina had voted him. North Carolina allowed him a percentage on all cotton gins used in that State for five years. Tennessee promised to do the same, but did not keep her promise.

Mr. Whitney struggled along, year after year, until he was convinced that he should never receive a just return for his invention. Seeing no way to gain a competence from the cotton gin he determined to continue the contest no longer, removed to New Haven and turned his attention to the making of firearms. Here he eventually gained a fortune. He made such improvements in the manufacture of firearms as to lay his country under permanent obligation to him for greatly increasing the means of national defense.

Robert Fulton once said: "Arkwright, Watt, and Whitney were the three men that did the most for mankind of any of their contemporaries." Macaulay said: "What Peter the Great did to make Russia dominant, Eli Whitney's invention of the cotton gin has more than equaled in its relation to the power and progress of the United States."

CHAPTER III.

COTTON.

ALMOST exactly in the center of England is the County of Derby. A few miles north of the city of Derby, on a small river called Derwent, a branch of the Trent, is the little town of Belper. This town was noted for its early manufacture of cotton and silk goods. Here, about the time of the American Revolution, Richard Arkwright and Jedediah Strutt were successfully engaged in cotton spinning.

In this town, in 1763, was born Samuel Slater. As the lad grew up, his father, a well-to-do farmer, sent him to school where he received the advantages of a good English education. His school days, however, ended when he was fourteen years of age. He was greatly interested in machinery. The hum of the spinning frame was music to his ears. Therefore, he was apprenticed to Mr. Strutt to learn the business of cotton spinning, and gained a thorough mastery of the process of carding and spinning cotton, and even while an apprentice he made many improvements in machinery.

At the close of the Revolutionary War, the Constitution of the United States was adopted and George Washington became President. We have already seen that England did not permit her American colonies to engage to any great extent in manufacturing. But now, the very first Congress under Washington passed an act to encourage manufactures, and one or two of the States offered bounties for the introduction of cotton machinery.

Young Slater, now about twenty-one years of age, determined to emigrate to America. Since the laws of England did not permit him to take drawings or models with him, he had to trust entirely to his memory to construct new machinery when he should arrive in this country. He landed in New York in November, 1789, and soon after wrote to Moses Brown, a wealthy merchant of Providence, Rhode Island, telling him what he could do and asking his help. Mr. Brown immediately replied: "If thou canst do this thing, I invite thee to come to Rhode Island and have the credit of introducing cotton manufactures into America."

So it happened that on the 21st of December, 1790, Samuel Slater, representing the business firm of "Almy, Brown and Slater," set up at Pawtucket three eighteen-inch carding machines, with the necessary drawing heads, roving cases, winders, and spinning frames, with seventy-two spindles. Here, in an old fulling mill, and by water power, was started machinery for the making of cotton yarn. Mr. Slater had been obliged to prepare all the plans of this machinery, and either to construct it with his own hands or to teach others how to do it. From the first the enterprise was successful. An excellent quality of yarn was manufactured, quite equal to the best quality then made in England. No attempts were made to use water power in weaving the yarn into cloth. This was still done by hand looms in the farmhouses of the country. A second cotton factory was started in the year 1800, and within ten years from that date there were many of them in different parts of the land.

When Mr. Slater came to America, he left at his father's house in Belper a little brother. In 1805 this brother, now grown to manhood, came to America, and went to Pawtucket to find his brother Samuel. Here he found Mr. Wilkinson, a brother-in-law of Mr. Slater. Mr. Wilkinson took him to his brother's house and said: "I have brought one of your countrymen to see you; can you find anything for him to do?" Mr. Slater asked from what part of England he came.

He replied: "Derbyshire."

"What part of Derbyshire?" said Mr. Slater.

"I came from the town of Belper," said John.

"Belper, the town of Belper? Well, that is where I came from. What may I call your name?"

"John Slater."

The boy had changed so much that his older brother did not know him. The interview was a delightful one to both; it was like the meeting of Joseph and Benjamin. Questions and answers flew rapidly.

"Is my mother yet alive? How are my brothers and sisters? How is my old master, Mr. Strutt? Is the old schoolmaster Jackson living?"

The next year the two brothers built a cotton mill in Smithfield, Rhode Island, and in 1808 a large stone mill was erected at Blackstone, Massachusetts.

So the business continued to increase. The power loom was invented, and soon the manufacture of cotton cloth became one of the leading interests of New England. The mills of Lowell became famous. Manchester, in New Hampshire, Lawrence and Fall River, in Massachusetts, were soon dotted with great mills turning out cloth of all varieties by the million yards. The falls upon the rivers of New England were utilized, by means of the water wheel, to furnish power for moving all the machinery used in the making of cotton goods. The song of the picker, the hum of the spinning frame, and the whack, whack of the loom are now heard in a thousand mills in various parts of our country.

Mr. Slater was visited at one time by Andrew Jackson while he was President. It is related that the following conversation took place between them:

"I understand," said the President, "that you have taught us how to spin so as to rival Great Britain and that it is you who have set all these thousands of spindles at work, which I have been so delighted to see, and which are making so many people happy by giving them employment."

"Yes sir," said Mr. Slater," I suppose that I gave out the Psalm, and they have been singing the tune ever since."

PRESIDENT JACKSON AND MR. SLATER.

THE INTERIOR OF A MODERN COTTON MILL.

Samuel Slater died in 1835, leaving a large fortune to his family. John Slater died a few years after the death of his brother. It was his son, John F. Slater, who in 1882 placed $1,000,000 in the hands of a board of trustees, the interest of which was to be used for the education of the freedmen of the South and their descendants. The great Rhode Island orator, Tristam Burgess, said in Congress on one occasion: "If manufacturing establishments are a benefit and a blessing to the Union, the name of Slater must ever be held in grateful remembrance by the American people."

It would be next to impossible to give any adequate account of the improvements which have been made in American machinery for the manufacture of cotton cloth. Beginning with the cotton gin and the introduction of the carding machine and the spinning frame by Slater, we should have to record the great success of the double speeder, the modern drawing-frame, the Crompton and the Whitin looms, and especially the ring traveler spinning frame and the self-operating cotton mule.

In 1791, 200,000 pounds of cotton were exported, very little being used in this country. In 1891, the cotton produced in America reached more than 3,500,000,000 pounds. This cotton is now grown in the Southern States upon more than 20,000,000 acres of ground. The mills of America to-day are using more than 2,000,000 bales of cotton per year. In 1793, Samuel Slater started seventy-two spindles to spin cotton; in 1893, there were 15,000,000 spindles. To such great proportions has this industry grown from the small beginnings of Samuel Slater's bold attempt to bring over from England in his memory the machinery necessary to its manufacture.

CHAPTER IV.

WOOL.

As civilization has advanced, the clothing of man has improved. To-day a great variety of material is necessary to make up the proper wardrobe for civilized man. Our clothing is nearly all fabricated—that is, manufactured from the raw material into what we call fabrics. We have cotton, woolen, silk, and linen fabrics. The two principal articles used for our clothing, however, are wool and cotton. Cotton and linen are more largely used in warm weather and in warm climates, while woolen has come into general use for wear in colder climates and in colder seasons.

The making of woolen cloth is one of the oldest industries. In the early ages the coarse wool of the sheep was spun into long threads, then woven and made into rude garments for the clothing of man. The dyeing of these cloths, by which brilliant colors were produced, was one of the earliest of the fine arts. Many centuries ago the Egyptians, the Persians, the Greeks, and the Romans made shawls and robes of beautiful texture and brilliant colors. They also made mats, rugs, tent cloths, curtains, and tapestry hangings.

During the last four hundred years steady progress has been made in the construction of woolen fabrics. Long ago England became famous for the manufacture of worsted goods, carpets, and broadcloths. Machinery for making woolen cloth was introduced into England during the latter half of the last century. The spinning jenny came into use a little after 1750, and the power loom was invented near the close of the century.

No machinery for making woolen cloth, except by hand spinning and hand weaving, was introduced into our country until about the year 1800. How do you suppose our forefathers and foremothers managed to make the cloth needed before the introduction of machinery and the building of factories? A single incident may explain how it was done.

Rev. Dr. Eliphalet Nott was president of Union College, Schenectady, New York, for more than sixty years. He was born in Connecticut just before the American Revolution. His father was very poor, but a conscientious, godly man. He lived on a farm four miles from the village and the church. During the early boyhood of Eliphalet his father had no horse, and in bad weather, when the family could not walk to church, they were drawn over the rough and hilly roads of that long four miles by their only cow. Yet they were always at church.

One winter, Mr. Nott's overcoat had become so shabby that Mrs. Nott told her husband it was not fit to be worn to church any longer. He had no money to buy a new one. Should he stay away from divine service? Not he! To this proposition neither he nor his wife would assent. Soon, however, the good woman devised a plan to free them from the difficulty. She suggested to her husband that they should shear their only "cosset" lamb, and that the fleece would furnish wool enough for a new overcoat.

"What!" said the old man, "shear the cosset in January? It will freeze."

"Ah, no, it will not," said the wife, "I will see to that; the lamb shall not suffer."

She sheared the cosset and then wrapped it in a blanket of burlaps, well sewed on, which kept it warm until its wool had grown again. This fleece Mrs. Nott carded, spun, and wove into cloth, which she cut and made into a garment for her husband, and he wore it to church on the following Sabbath.

The first attempt to manufacture woolen cloth other than by hand was made at Newburyport, Massachusetts, by two Englishmen, Arthur and John Scholfield. They had learned the business in England, and now put in operation the first carding machine for wool made in the United States. Upon this they made the first spinning rolls turned out by machinery. The same year they built a factory, three stories high and one hundred feet long, in the Byfield district, at Newburyport. The two brothers carried on the factory for a company of gentlemen who were the stockholders. Arthur was overseer of the carding; John was in charge of the weaving room.

This application of machinery to the making of woolen cloth created much interest in the country, and wool was brought from long distances. People visited the factory from far and near. These visitors became so numerous that an admission fee of ten cents was charged. During the first winter after the factory was opened sleighing parties came from all the neighboring towns.

Some years ago an old lady, ninety years of age, wrote, in "Reminiscences of a Nonagenarian," that she had seen row after row of sleighs pass over Crane-neck Hill, enlivening the bright cold days by the joyous tones of their merry bells. She describes the impression made upon her own mind the first time she visited the factory: "Never shall I forget the awe with which I entered what then appeared the vast and imposing edifice. The large drums that carried the bands on the lower floor, coupled with the novel noise and hum, increased this awe, but when I reached the second floor where picking, carding, spinning, and weaving were in process, my amazement became complete. The machinery, with the exception of the looms, was driven by water power. The weaving was by hand. Most of the operatives were males, a few young girls being employed in splicing rolls."

After this John Scholfield established a factory in Montville, Connecticut. Subsequently Arthur Scholfield removed to Pittsfield, Massachusetts, where he passed the remainder of his life, and not only carried on the woolen manufacture himself, but also built carding machines and set them up for others to operate. Within the next twelve years several woolen factories had been built in Massachusetts, New Hampshire, Rhode Island, and New York.

The new industry had become so firmly established that when President

Madison was inaugurated, March 4, 1809, he wore a suit of black broadcloth of American manufacture. But Washington Irving tells us that Washington, our first president, was inaugurated twenty years earlier, dressed in a "suit of dark-brown cloth of American manufacture."

From time to time the woolen industry has been protected by various tariff bills passed by Congress. This industry to-day is of gigantic proportions. The woolen factories in our country are now using about five hundred million pounds of wool per year. More than half of this is raised in our own country, and nearly all of the cloth produced is retained in the country for home consumption.

Let us see now if we can understand how woolen cloth is made. The father of Dr. Nott had in those early days a single sheep. Some farmers would have half a dozen, others twenty-five or fifty. Now times are changed. We have but few sheep in the older settled country along the Atlantic coast. Those who raise wool to-day are apt to make it their sole business, doing nothing else. Most of the sheep of this country are raised upon the great plains and in the great valleys of the Western country.

Many flocks of sheep, numbering from five hundred to several thousand, may be seen in Texas, New Mexico, Utah, and Wyoming. There are to-day in Texas more than three million sheep; about an equal number in Wyoming; nearly as many in New Mexico, Oregon, California, and Ohio. We have in our country at the present time more than forty million sheep.

SHEEP-SHEARING.

Let us visit one of these sheep ranches. It is in the spring of the year. The warm weather has come. The sheep have had their thick fleeces to keep them warm through the cold winter. In the summer these thick, shaggy coats would be as burdensome to them as a winter overcoat would be to us. The ranchmen round up the flock, and taking them one by one, cut off with a huge pair of shears the long wool.

The wool is sold to the dealers, and sent away to the market. It finds its way to the woolen mill. It is sorted, washed, and scoured. It is then carded. The cards straighten out the long fibres of wool so that they may be readily spun. The mule or the spinning jenny spins it into yarn, twisting this yarn like a rope or thread so that it will be strong and will hold together. A part of the yarn is then arranged upon a great beam for the warp. The warp is the threads that run lengthwise of the cloth. The rest of it is wound upon little bobbins to be put into shuttles. The shuttle is thrown back and forth across the warp, thus weaving in the filling. This is done by means of what is called a harness. This harness holds up the alternate threads of the warp and presses down the other threads, so that when the shuttle is thrown through it carries the thread of the filling "under and over"; that is, under one-half of the warp threads and over the other half.

After the cloth is woven, it is put through the fulling mill, which beats it up thick and firm. After this come the various processes of finishing: shearing the surface so as to leave it smooth; brushing it so as to set the nap all one way and give it a smooth, even, glossy appearance. The quality of the cloth depends upon the quality of the wool used, the quality of the machinery which makes the cloth, and the skill of the workmen. A great deal of experience is necessary in making first-class goods.

We are now using the very best machinery in the world in the manufacture of our woolen goods. Possibly in the making of broadcloth and a few varieties of the better class of goods we may not yet be quite up to the older manufactories of Europe, but in cassimeres, worsted goods, blankets and carpets we are already able to compete with the products of the Old World. Although the price of labor in European countries is less than in America, our workmen do more work in a day and our machinery is of such improved patterns that we are generally able to compete in price.

CHAPTER V.

LEATHER.

In the colonial days, as we have seen, the traveling shoemaker was abroad in the land. He was accustomed to travel through his section of the country with a kit of tools and bits of leather on his back. He was familiarly called "Crispin," from the patron saint of his craft, and ofttimes proved a "character" much appreciated by the farmers and their families. Sometimes these traveling mechanics were quiet, silent men, doing their work and going on intent only on obtaining their living; but sometimes they were jolly, social people, facetious, even witty.

"Good mornin', neighbor Heyday," said a Crispin to a farmer. "I hope you and the madam and the childers are all very well, the day."

"Eh, purty fair. The woman is ailin' some. She wants buildin' up, buildin' up."

"Well, well," said Crispin, "the Lord has laid His hand of blessing heavily upon ye, so He has that."

"What is the meanin' of that speech?" said the farmer.

"Eh, sorry is it for the joker when he has to explain his own joke. Hasn't He filled your quiver full of childers? and isn't that the greatest blessing the Almighty can bestow on man that is a sinner?"

"But I have only six childers."

"Yes, yes, I see, but the eldest counts less years than the clock tell hours; and I wish ye had a dozen instead of half as many. Are ye givin' 'em all good healthy understandin'?"

"Well, them that's old enough goes to school, if that's what you mean?"

"Well, there it is again. A man has to interpret his own wit. I mean, have they all good soles on which to keep their bodies healthy?"

"The good Lord gives 'em the souls and their parents are responsible only for the bodies."

"Blunderin' again it is that I am. I mean are ye'r shoes all in a good, healthy condition, so that the brats will not take cold and be carried off by a stout, lung fever, that the doctors call newmony?"

"Well, they've worn no shoes all summer except what the Lord gave 'em, and that's the skin of their feet."

"Well, now, it's a full twelvemonth since I was around here afore, and do ye want me to make up their winter shoes for 'em?"

So the conversation went on until they had struck a bargain, that the Crispin should board with the farmer and make up the shoes for himself and the children, the farmer paying for the leather and so much by the week for the man's work. The shoemaker then made a strong pair of cowhide boots for the father of the family; a pair of kid shoes for the good wife; two pairs of calfskin shoes for the two girls; two pairs of ingrain boots for the older boys; and two pairs of kid shoes for the younger boys. The silver jingled in the pocket of the Crispin when his task was completed, and he traveled onward to the next farm. He had appropriated to himself a certain section of villages and country, and he would treat the matter as a serious misdemeanor should any other Crispin trespass upon his territory.

The Crispins of those days were honest and faithful in their work. Slow they were,—that cannot be denied. Even as late as the early half of this century a good shoemaker has been known to labor from morning till night through the six days of the week on one pair of fine, sewed, calfskin boots, and the entire price which the customer paid for them was $5, which included both labor and material.

What a contrast from the ancient method the present system furnishes! Not long since a wedding was to occur in Salem, Massachusetts. A telegram was sent at ten o'clock in the morning to Lynn, ordering a pair of ladies' slippers made from white kid, to be worn at the ceremony that afternoon. The shoes were cut out and made up complete and forwarded to Salem by the two o'clock train.

Miss Sarah E. Wiltse in her stories for children tells how little Alice was drinking her cup of milk one night when she asked her father to tell her a story about the good cow, for her third finger. She said: "The cow does three things for me now. Here is milk for my thumb, butter for the pointer, cheese for Mr. Tallman, and now my third finger, Mr. Feebleman, wants something. What can the cow give me for my third finger?"

Her father then told her the story of a king in the long, long ago,—I think it must have been in the pre-historic times,—a king who put into one pile the things which he knew, and into another pile the things which he did not know. Now the pile which this foolish king did not know was a great deal larger than the pile of things which he did know. Neither he nor his people knew much about making houses or dishes or even clothes for themselves. They went barefooted and bareheaded all the time. One day the king's horse fell dead and he was obliged to walk a long distance. The sharp stones cut his feet, and the briars and brambles pricked them and tore them. Then the king told his people to put down a carpet for him to walk on. So they all went to work to make coarse carpets for the king to walk upon.

They had hard work to make carpets enough to lay down in advance of the king, day after day, as he traveled across the country. At length one of his servants went away by himself and worked all night. The next morning he came and knelt before the king and said:

"Sire, I have a carpet for the whole earth, though none but the king may walk upon it. Upon this carpet thou canst climb mountains and thy feet be not bruised; thou canst wander in the valleys and thy feet never be torn by brambles; thou canst tread the burning desert and thy feet remain unscorched."

Then the king said: "Bring me that priceless carpet and half my kingdom shall be thine." The servant brought to the king a pair of shoes which he had made in the night. This was a new carpet for the king; and so this was the fourth good thing which the cow gave to Alice; the milk she put down for the thumb, the butter for the first finger, the cheese for the middle finger, and now she put leather for the third finger. What great changes have taken place in the process of making boots and shoes since this witty servant made the carpet for the king's feet!

Let us trace briefly the history of leather and the evolution of a pair of shoes. In the early colonial days the skins of animals were widely used for clothing. Caps were made for the men and boys from bear skins, wolf skins, and the skins of the catamount. Overcoats with sleeves and hoods were made of skins of wild animals properly dressed, with the hair on. Moccasins for winter service were from the same material. Buckskin breeches with fringed edges were in common use. These costumes in the newly settled regions of our Western country continued until fifty or sixty years ago.

DR. WHITMAN STARTING ON HIS JOURNEY.

In the winter of 1842-43 Dr. Marcus Whitman made his memorable journey from Oregon across the country to the States. On a later occasion he described the dress which he wore on that remarkable horseback ride. He said: "I wore buckskin breeches, fur moccasins, a blue duffle coat, a buffalo overcoat with hood, and a bearskin cap. Rather a fantastic garb for a missionary, wasn't it?"

Inventions and machinery have done much to improve the processes of tanning leather. Tanning itself is a curious process. It changes raw hides into a condition in which the skins are useful in the arts and manufactures. This process renders the skins nearly impervious to water, and makes them so tough that they can withstand the ravages of time and remain firm and strong even for centuries.

It is said that specimens of leather have been discovered in China which are surely three thousand years old. They had been tanned by the process which is called "alum tannage." When Columbus discovered America he found, in possession of the Indians, skins that had been tanned. Their process of tanning, too, was practically the alum method.

Sir Edwin Arnold found a pair of slippers in a sarcophagus in India, and nothing else was present except a small heap of dust. In the huts of the Rock Dwellers in Arizona tanned leather has been found. In ancient Babylon they had a process of tanning, and nearly two thousand years ago the Russians and Hungarians were skilled in the art. The ancient Romans knew how to tan leather with oil, alum, and bark.

Most of the early tanning, however, was without bark. The process was accomplished with oil, clay, sour milk, and smoke. Later, nutgalls and leaves began to be used. Oak bark is the principal material now employed throughout the world in tanning. Besides the oak bark, the barks of hemlock, pine, birch, and willow are utilized.

When the texture of the skin has been so changed by this tanning process as to become tough and durable, then the name leather is given to it. In the days of the Crispins six months was as short a time as the tanner thought needful for the proper curing of the hides. The process was crude, long, and laborious; but the leather, ah! the leather—it was strong and would wear like iron. Even the children did not need copper toes. To-day the methods have changed greatly; in no way more noticeably than in the shorter time required. The modern process must be considered an improvement, even though the leather is not as strong as formerly.

The skins of most animals may be used to make leather The domestic animals, cows, calves, and sheep, are first called upon to give their skins for leather. Glazed kid is made from goat skins. Kangaroo leather is much used for shoes. Considerable use is made of alligator leather for satchels and bags and even for shoes. Skins of lizards, snakes, and seals are used; walrus hides are tanned, and the leather used for polishing knives and tools. "Patent leather" is made principally of cowhide, horsehide, and calfskin. Horsehide leather is very tough and durable, but is too elastic for some purposes. Harness leather is made from steer and cow hides. "Russia leather," formerly made only in Russia, has been a favorite material for the choicest kinds of pocketbooks and satchels. Bookbinders prefer it for binding their most costly volumes.

Marshall Jewell was a New Hampshire boy. He learned the trade of tanning and worked at it with his father. While yet a young man, he removed to Hartford, Connecticut. There, at first with his father and afterward alone, he carried on a large business in manufacturing leather belting. He was three times governor of the State. The year after leaving the governor's chair he was appointed Minister to Russia. While in that country, through his intimate knowledge of the methods of tanning, he discovered the secret of the Russian process. It had never been known before in our country. Under his direction it was introduced here, and within the last twenty-five years it has come into very extensive use. The process is quite simple. It is thus described: Steep the leather in a solution of fifty pounds each of oak and hemlock bark and sumach, one pound of willow bark and nine hundred gallons of water; heat by steam, and immerse the leather till struck through, and while the material is still damp smear on the outer side a solution of oil of birch bark dissolved in a little alcohol and ether. This imparts to the leather its odor and its pliability.

A boot or shoe consists principally of two parts: the sole, made of thick, tough, strong leather, and the uppers, made of a softer, more pliable leather. By the old process the boot or the shoe was made throughout by a single person. By the modern process, one person cuts out the shoe, another binds it, and a third puts it upon the last; still another manages the machine which sews the sole and the upper together, a different person trims the edges, some one else attends to the next process in the division of labor, until, it may be, a dozen persons have done something to the making of one shoe.

The modern improved machines for sewing on the soles of shoes are wonderful instruments. Upon one machine a good workman will sew eight hundred pairs of women's shoes in ten hours. A great part of the boots and shoes worn by the people of this country are made with this improved machinery in large establishments in New York, Philadelphia, Baltimore, and other large cities, and particularly in several towns in Massachusetts, New Hampshire, and Maine. The most important seat of this manufacture is Lynn, Massachusetts, but great quantities of shoes are made in Brockton, Haverhill, Milford, Marblehead, Danvers, and Worcester in Massachusetts, Portland, Auburn, and Augusta in Maine, and Dover and Farmington, in New Hampshire.

CHAPTER VI.

NEEDLES.

In the earlier times what was the mantle that covered the human person? How was it made? How was it held together? With what was the sewing thereof? When was thread first used for the seam? How early in human history was the eye made for the needle?

From the beginning of history we find references to sewing, even earlier than to weaving. We might naturally suppose that leather was sewed before cloth, and that stout leathern thongs served for thread. The leather string for thread and the awl for the needle must have been in use long, long ago. The stout moccasin, the wolfskin cap, the buckskin breeches were sewed by punching holes and laboriously pulling a leather string through them. By and by, however, some skillful inventor produced the needle. Perhaps the first needles were made of bone or ivory. Then metal was used.

What a great invention was the eye of the needle! No one knows who was the inventor, but we have reason to bless the unknown personage who first devised this ingenious arrangement. Would you not like to see the needles that were in use hundreds of years ago? They were not like the finely finished needles of to-day. Crude and coarse were they, and only adapted to the crude and coarse sewing which could then be performed. To-day the needle-woman is often an artist. Embroidery is done with the needle. The plain seam, the hem, the gather, the back stitch, are simply so many forms of the work of an artist.

Century after century our needle-makers have been improving in the manufacture of this simple but effective little machine. In the complicated civilization of the present time we have an almost infinite variety of needles: the ordinary sewing needle for the making of garments; smaller needles for lace work, the hemming of delicate handkerchiefs and the seam of fine silk goods; and coarse and heavy needles for carpet sewing, bagging, and leather work.

All this relates to sewing by hand, with a single needle and one thread. It is stitch by stich, first one, then another; it is like the brook,—"it goes on forever." It is like the clock that repeats its tick tock, tick tock by the hour, by the day, by the week, by the year. Perhaps many seamstresses would not recognize the duty of blessing the man who invented the needle. The poet Hood has told this side of the story in his famous poem, "The Song of the Shirt."

"With fingers weary and worn.
With eyelids heavy and red,

A woman sits in unwomanly rags,
Plying her needle and thread—
Stitch! Stitch! Stitch!
In poverty, hunger, and dirt.

· · · · ·

Work! Work! Work!
While the cock is crowing aloof!
And work—work—work,
Till the stars shine through the roof!

· · · · ·

Band and gusset and seam,
Seam and gusset and band,
Till the heart is sick,
And the brain benumbed
As well as the weary hand."

SEWING BY HAND.

Indeed, the time had come long ago when some ingenious device was needed by which the seamstress could sew with less wear and tear of nerve and muscle. Efforts were made sin England for machine sewing nearly one hundred and fifty years ago, but they were not successful. A sewing machine was invented by Thomas Saint about one hundred years ago which had some of the features of the sewing machine of to-day.

It was left, however, for American inventors to produce machines that would do the work easily and successfully; the machines themselves had such simplicity and were so nicely adapted that they were not likely to get out of repair but would remain serviceable during a long period of years. Sewing machines in large numbers were invented during the period from 1830 to 1860.

As early as 1818 a sewing machine was invented by Rev. John Adams Dodge, of Vermont. He used a needle pointed at each end with the eye in the middle. This machine would make a good backstitch and sew a seam straight forward. It was not patented and did not get into use to any considerable extent. In 1832 Walter Hunt, of New York, brought out a machine which used two threads, one being carried by a shuttle and the other by a curved needle with the eye in the point. This machine also was not patented.

Ten years later, J. J. Greenough patented a machine for sewing leather and other heavy material, but this also did not acquire any extended use. About the same time George H. Corliss invented a strong, heavy machine for sewing leather, using two needles with the eyes near the points; this machine was evidently an improvement on previous attempts. Mr. Corliss soon turned his attention to improvements of the steam engine and did not continue his efforts to perfect his sewing machine.

Hence it was that the first really successful sewing machine was that of Elias Howe, patented in 1846. The first form of Howe's machine was far from satisfactory, but it was an improvement on all previous machines. Howe could not induce the people to appreciate the value of his invention, and he went to England and there secured patents. But in England also he became discouraged, and sold out his rights for that country and returned home.

Meantime others had pirated his invention and were making his machines and placing them upon the market. Howe immediately asserted his rights and, after a series of suits in court, he succeeded in establishing them, so that finally his machine came into extended use and its inventor reaped a large pecuniary reward from his genius and skill. Improvements now came forward rapidly. Patents were soon issued to Allen B. Wilson of Pittsfield, Massachusetts, Isaac M. Singer of New York, and William O. Grover of Boston. Later, the Weed, the Florence, the Wilcox & Gibbs, the Remington, Domestic, American, Household, and many others were added to the list of successful machines.

It is unnecessary to describe the difference in these machines and the various ways in which the stitch is made. Some of them make the lock stitch, others the double loop stitch, and still others the single chain stitch. The best machines make also a special buttonhole stitch and have particular devices by which they gather and ruffle, tuck, hem, bind, and whatever else is required to be done with thread.

One machine or another can be used for almost any kind of sewing. With them we sew shoes and boots, heavy woolen goods like beaver, several thicknesses of duck, or, on the other hand, the very finest and nicest muslin. Sewing machines are used in the making of gloves, pocketbooks, traveling bags, and other articles of this character. Special machines sew seams on water hose, leather buckets, bootlegs, and other articles which require the seam to be made in a circle.

No other country has so many factories or such large ones for making sewing machines as the United States. The establishments which manufacture sewing machines have a combined capital of more than twenty million dollars, and the value of their annual product aggregates about fifteen million dollars. Meanwhile the price of sewing machines has diminished so that they are now sold for less than one-half, and sometimes as low as one-fourth, of the original price.

In 1830 a Frenchman, Barthélemy Thimmonier, constructed of wood eighty machines which made a chain stitch of great strength. These were used for making clothing for the French army. Laborers were so incensed at this invention, which they thought was contrary to their interests, that they raised a riot and destroyed all of the machines. A few years later this inventor made other machines constructed of metal, and these were also destroyed by a mob.

Many times it has happened that laborers have supposed that they would be great losers from the invention of labor-saving machines. Instead of this proving to be true, it would seem that laborers are benefited by the inventions. There is much evidence showing that while inventions greatly diminish the amount of labor necessary to accomplish a certain result, on the other hand they open up new lines of industry which fully compensate laborers for the loss which would otherwise fall upon them. It is to be noted also that, in our country at least, the wages of laborers have increased in the period during which labor-saving machines have been invented.

The modern sewing machine is an inestimable blessing to a family. In former days, the mother of half a dozen children would be obliged to ply the needle night after night until the small hours in order to keep her little ones properly clad. Now, with the little iron machine standing upon its small table on one side of the room, the good mother can make up the necessary garments for her children in quick time, leaving her far more hours for sleep, recreation, and social life than would be possible under the old method. Many a one can now call down blessings not only upon "the man who invented sleep," but upon the man who invented the sewing machine which gives one time to sleep.

CHAPTER VII.

THE STEAM ENGINE.

AT the very summit of a mountain near Pasadena, California, stands a huge windmill, which may be seen for many miles in all directions. Here the wind blows almost constantly, and the great arms of the windmill are employed to lift water from a well in the valley below to irrigate the orange groves on the hillsides. Thus the wind has been harnessed by man to serve his purpose.

AN OLD WINDMILL.

Nature has not only furnished wind for a motive force, but it has also provided man with water power. The water wheel, with its accompanying dam across the stream, has been in general use from the time of the earliest settlements. The weight of the water turned a wheel, thus developing a force which was employed for sawing lumber or grinding grain. When cotton and woolen manufactories were first introduced, water power was almost universally used.

After wind and water came steam. A very simple steam engine was devised by

Hero more than two thousand years ago, but it was of little practical value and was soon forgotten. Not until the beginning of the eighteenth century was a machine invented which could successfully produce motion by steam. This engine, made by an Englishman named Newcomen, was very wasteful and was used only to pump water from mines.

Less than one hundred and fifty years ago a young Scotchman named James Watt set himself to the task of improving the Newcomen engine and of making a steam engine that would furnish power for different purposes. He devoted his whole thought to his work, and after twenty years of study he succeeded. The Watt steam engine is the basis of all engines to-day. James Watt did not discover steam power, but he made the steam engine of real value.

Many of the first engines used in this country for manufacturing purposes were made by Boulton and Watt in Birmingham. The first steam engines made in America were rough and crude, but the improvement in their construction was rapid. At the present time engines of the finest construction, with the latest improvements and adapted to all kinds of work, are made in many establishments all over our land. Engines are made for marine purposes—steamboats, yachts, and war-vessels,—stationary engines for all sorts of manufactures, and locomotives for the railroads. Perhaps the greatest improvements in the manufacture of steam engines have been the result of the talent and genius of George H. Corliss.

In 1825, when George was only eight years of age, his father moved to Greenwich, New York, where the boy grew up to manhood. Here he went to school, was clerk in a country store, and was employed in the first cotton factory built in that State. Little did the people of that country village think that this quiet boy had in him such wonderful mechanical genius as he afterward displayed.

His father's house was situated near the bank of a small stream which was much swollen every springtime by the freshets from the melting snows above. A bridge which spanned this stream was carried away one year by the freshets. Young Corliss, then twenty-one years of age, proposed to build a cantilever bridge. Everybody said that the scheme was impossible; he could not do it, it would be a failure. Nevertheless he succeeded, and the bridge was built. It proved entirely successful. It withstood the freshets and was in service, scarcely needing repairs, for many years.

He went to Providence when he was twenty-seven years of age, and before he was thirty he had established himself as the head of the firm of "Corliss, Nightingale and Company," for the manufacture of steam engines. He was but a little over thirty years old when he patented his great improvements, applied to the steam engine. These improvements were such as to produce uniformity of motion and to prevent the loss of steam. By connecting the valve with an ingenious cut-off, which he invented, he made the engine work with such uniformity that, if all but one of a hundred looms in a factory were suddenly stopped, that one would go on working at the same rate of speed as before.

The improvements which Mr. Corliss effected at once revolutionized the construction of the steam engine. He immediately began the erection of immense buildings for his machine shops, where now are employed more than a thousand men. In 1856 the "Corliss Steam Engine Company" was incorporated, and Mr. Corliss, purchasing the interest of his partners, soon owned all the stock of this company and was both president and treasurer. During a long period of more than forty years Mr. Corliss, who was a large-hearted, benevolent man interested in public affairs relating to city, State, and nation, devoted himself with great industry to the development of his inventions.

A CORLISS ENGINE.

Perhaps the most conspicuous work which more than anything else carried his name to all the nations of the earth was the construction of the great engine which furnished the motive power for all the machinery in operation in Machinery Hall, at the Centennial Exhibition in Philadelphia in 1876. Of this engine M. Bartholdi, in his report to the French Government, said: "It belonged to the category of works of art by the general beauty of its effect and its perfect balance to the eye." Professor Radinger, of the Polytechnic School in Vienna, pronounced the engine one of the greatest works of the day.

This engine stood in the center of Machinery Hall upon a platform 56 feet in diameter. The two working beams were 40 feet above the platform, and were seen from all parts of the building, being the most conspicuous objects in the hall. The fly-wheel was 30 feet in diameter with a face of 24 inches.

This engine carried eight main lines of shafting, each line being 650 feet in length, and the larger part of this shafting was speeded to 120 revolutions a minute, while one line, used principally for wood-working machines, made 240 revolutions per minute. The engine weighed 7,000 tons, and its power was equivalent to 1,400 horse-power. The entire cost, about $200,000, was borne by Mr. Corliss. The engine is now in active service, furnishing the motive power for the entire works of the Pullman Car Company.

During the later years of Mr. Corliss's life he devoted much time and thought to inventing improved pumps to be used in connection with city waterworks, "for forcing water to higher levels." He made for the city of Providence a rotary pump for high service which worked automatically, keeping the pipes in the upper sections of the city full at all times whether much or little water was used. This ingenious pump was visited by mechanics from all parts of the world. Only a few years before his death Mr. Corliss built another pump, an account of which was published some years ago. This account included the following incident:

"I went down to Pettaconsett, the other day, to see the foundations of the building that Mr. Corliss is putting up there for the new pumping engine which he has engaged to put in for this city. I found that, in digging for the foundations, they came upon a deep bed of quicksand. Mr. Corliss, ever fertile in expedients to overcome obstacles, instead of driving down wooden piles, sunk in this quicksand great quantities of large cobblestones. These were driven down into the sand with tremendous force by a huge iron ball weighing four thousand pounds. I said: 'Mr. Corliss, why did not you drive wooden piles on which to build your foundation?'

"'Don't you see,' said he, 'that the piles *have no discretion*, and that the cobblestones have?'

"'I don't think I understand you, Mr. Corliss,' was my reply.

"'If you drive a pile,' said he, '*it goes where you drive it, and nowhere else*; but a cobblestone will seek the softest place and *go where it is most needed*. It therefore has discretion, and better answers the purpose.'

"I went away musing that the wooden 'piles' and the 'cobblestones' represent two classes of boys. 'The piles,' said Mr. Corliss, 'have *no discretion*, and *go only where they are driven*.' I think I have seen boys who represented this quality. 'But the cobblestones go *where they are the most needed*.' When boys fit themselves to go where they are the most needed, they will be pretty likely to meet with tolerably good success in life."

The great service Mr. Corliss has rendered to the world through his inventions is shown by the awards made to him from the highest scientific authorities. At the Paris Exposition (1867) he received the highest competitive prize in competition with more than a hundred engines. A great English engineer, one of the British commissioners at the Exposition, said: "The American engine of Mr. Corliss everywhere tells of wise forethought, judicious proportion, sound execution, and exquisite contrivance."

The American Academy of Arts and Sciences in 1870 awarded to Mr. Corliss the Rumford Medal. This medal was presented by Dr. Asa Gray, who said: "No invention since Watt's time has so enhanced the efficiency of the steam engine as this."

At the Vienna Exhibition in 1873 Mr. Corliss sent neither engine nor machinery, nor had he any one there to represent him; but the grand diploma of honor was awarded to him. This was done because foreign builders had sent their engines, which they themselves claimed were built on his system, and they had placed his name on their productions.

The steam engine to-day is of vastly greater importance than it has ever been before, especially in its use for furnishing the motive power for cotton and woolen factories, and for all kinds of manufacturing establishments. What should we do to-day without the steam engine? Long before the beginning of this century Erasmus Darwin sang as follows:

> "Soon shall thy arm, unconquered steam! afar
> Drag the slow barge, or drive the rapid car."

All this has long been fulfilled. How long will it be before his next two lines will also prove a reality?

> Or on wide-waving wings expanded bear
> The flying chariot through the field of air."

ROBERT FULTON.

AN OCEAN STEAMER.

"I carry the wealth and the lord of earth, the thoughts of his godlike mind;
The wind lags after my going forth, the lightning is left behind."

SECTION V.
TRAVEL.

CHAPTER I.

BY LAND.

"Well, Charles, how do you purpose to go to the city to-day? The paper this morning contains some news that ought to interest you. There was a washout at Turk's Bridge last evening, and it will be several hours yet before trains can run."

This question was asked by Mrs. Barlow, one morning during the great street-car strike when the motormen and conductors had refused to run cars until their demands were granted.

"I see but one way left open for me," replied her husband. "The roads must be very muddy, and I cannot go on my bicycle. I suppose that I shall be compelled to walk. That was the original mode of traveling, and I imagine that in this case of necessity I can try it again. I am not used to so long a walk, but I see no other way. In one respect I am better off than my ancestors were, for I have good level side-walks, most of them paved, instead of rough paths, partly trodden down. I will start to walk, anyway."

Mr. Barlow did not own a horse, and could not drive to the city. He did not feel able to hire a public carriage, as, since the street-car strike began, so many desired to ride that the drivers charged very high prices. But he felt that he must attend to his business in the city that day, and immediately after breakfast he started on his five-mile walk. He was very tired before he reached the office, and the walk home in the afternoon wearied him still more. He was therefore greatly pleased the next morning to find that the strike was over, the railroad bridge repaired, the muddy roads nearly dry, and a choice open to him to travel either by steam cars, electric street cars, or bicycle.

Mr. Barlow learned an interesting lesson by this one day's experience. He obtained something of an idea of the life of his ancestors, who were compelled to walk whenever they had business to transact. He realized more than ever before what improvements had been made in the last three centuries in the means for travel. His thoughts were turned directly to these changes, and for several weeks he studied histories and scientific works to learn the ways in which these improvements came about. Let us note some of the results of his study.

Nearly three hundred years ago, Captain Newport, with a few small vessels, sailed up the James River, in Virginia. After some weeks the fleet returned to England, leaving about one hundred men, the colonists of Jamestown, the first permanent English settlement in America. Here was a little village, with the Atlantic Ocean, thousands of miles wide, separating the colonists from all their friends and acquaintances. The great forest which covered the entire Atlantic coast contained now this clearing on the banks of the James River. North of the settlement dense woods extended in every direction; no white men lived nearer than the French colonies of Quebec and Nova Scotia. To the south also spread the forest; the nearest European settlement was the Spanish colony of Saint Augustine. Westward for hundreds and thousands of miles the almost uninhabited wilderness extended to the Pacific Ocean, the very existence of which was scarcely suspected by white men. Thus was the Jamestown colony almost entirely shut off from the world of civilization, a feeble band of Europeans surrounded by savage red men.

What interest had these colonists in travel? Tossed on the ocean as they had been for many weeks, worn with seasickness and lack of nourishing food, few had any desire to see more of the world. Besides, if they had wished to travel, where could they have gone? Roads through the forests were unknown; rivers were spanned by no bridges; swamps and marshes extended in every direction. The most remote houses were at easy walking distance. The little church was not far even from the last house in the village. If need for firewood or lumber led any one into the forest, he must go afoot. If any necessity arose for communication with the Indians, the journey must be made on foot. Thus we see that in the early days of Virginia what travel there was by land was limited to walking.

Thirteen years after the building of Jamestown a second English colony was planted in America. Another band of a hundred persons began a settlement at Plymouth in New England. The colony of Virginia had become well established by this time, yet it could be of but little help to Plymouth. Many hundred miles distant, it seemed hardly nearer than old England itself. The Pilgrims at Plymouth lived by themselves, as had the Virginia colonists, and for some years what travel they had was also on foot.

Time passed on in both colonies. New settlers came over the ocean to Virginia, and other villages were built at some distance from Jamestown. Thus arose reasons for journeys—desire to see friends in other villages—necessities of trade or commerce between the settlements. At first, of course, as travel by foot within a village was common, so journeys between villages were made in the same way.

An easier means of communication was provided when horses were brought over from England. These came in small numbers at first; there were but six horses in Virginia when the settlers had been there nine years. Thousands of years ago wild horses ranged in great numbers over the whole continent of America. But, for some reason or other, these had all perished, and when Columbus discovered the new world the red men were wholly unacquainted with these animals or their use. Therefore, when the white settlers in America desired horses they found it necessary to bring them in vessels from Europe.

To the first and most common mode of travel, by foot, was thus added the second method, namely, on horseback. In the old world this use of horses had existed for thousands of years. In fact, three hundred and four hundred years ago, at the time of the discovery and settlement of America, it was almost the universal means for land travel. It was natural then that it should be the first form taken up in America. Besides, the making of a bridle path through the woods, that is, a path wide enough for a man on horseback, was a comparatively simple matter. To build a carriage road would have been a much more difficult task.

In New England, as well as in Virginia, the population rapidly increased. The Plymouth colonists began to build other villages. A new colony was founded on the coast of Massachusetts Bay, but thirty miles from Plymouth. Here were established the towns of Salem, Charlestown, Roxbury, Dorchester, Newtown, and Boston. Other towns were soon built and clearings were made in every direction. Travel by horseback became common among those who could afford to keep horses. Those who were too poor must still travel on foot.

A MAN AND HIS WIFE TRAVELING ON HORSEBACK.

Most of the traveling was done by men. We read that Queen Elizabeth was an accomplished horsewoman; but as a rule few women were accustomed to hold the reins, and few side-saddles were in use. The horses of those days were very strong. They were trained to carry heavy burdens on their backs rather than to draw loaded wagons. They frequently carried more than one person; it was not unusual to see a man riding horseback, and behind him his wife, sitting sideways and holding on to her husband to keep from slipping off. For her comfort a pillion was used, which was a pad or cushion fastened to the saddle.

Not only was Massachusetts Bay rapidly settled, but villages were built fifty and even a hundred miles from Boston. Providence, Newport, and Portsmouth were founded, forming the colony of Rhode Island and Providence Plantations. Hartford, Wethersfield, and Windsor were established on the Connecticut. Dover and Portsmouth in New Hampshire, New Haven and Saybrook in Connecticut were built, and the village of Agawam, now Springfield, was founded.

All of these new settlements needed some connection with Boston, or the Old Bay Colony as it was called. The roads were mere paths, however, and over them carriages could not have passed, if there had been any. In a story written by J. G. Holland, called "Bay-Path," he described life in Agawam more than two and a half centuries ago, and his description of the roads and travel in those days is well worth reading.

"The principal communication with the Eastern settlement was by a path marked by trees a portion of the distance, and by slight clearings of brush and thicket for the remainder. No stream was bridged, no hill graded, and no marsh drained. The path led through woods which bore the marks of centuries, and along the banks of streams that the seine had never dragged. The path was known as 'the Bay-Path,' or the path to the bay.

THE BAY-PATH.

"It was wonderful what a powerful interest was attached to the Bay-Path. It was the channel through which laws were communicated, through which flowed news from distant friends, and through which came long, loving letters and messages. That rough thread of soil, chopped by the blades of a hundred streams, was a bond that radiated at each terminus into a thousand fibers of love and interest and hope and memory.

"The Bay-Path was charmed ground—a precious passage—and during the spring, the summer, and the early autumn hardly a settler at Agawam went out of doors or changed his position in the fields, or looked up from his labor, or rested his oars upon the bosom of the river, without turning his eyes to the point at which that path opened from the brow of the wooded hill upon the East. And when some worn and wearied man came in sight upon his half-starved horse, or two or three pedestrians, bending beneath their packs and swinging their sturdy staves, were seen approaching, the village was astir from one end to the other.

"The Bay-Path became better marked from year to year as settlements began to string themselves upon it as upon a thread. Every year the footsteps of those who trod it hurried more and more until, at last, wheels began to be heard upon it—heavy carts creaking with merchandise. A century passed away and the wilderness had retired. There was a constant roll along the Bay-Path. The finest of the wheat and the fattest of the flocks and herds were transported to the Bay, whose young commerce had already begun to whiten the coast.

"The dreamy years passed by, and then came the furious stagecoach, traveling night and day—splashing the mud, brushing up the dust, dashing up to inns, and curving more slowly up to post-offices. The journey was reduced to a day. And then—miracle of miracles—came the railway and the locomotive. The journey of a day is reduced to three hours."

CHAPTER II.

BY WATER.

When the Virginia colonists reached the shores of America, they sailed up the James River until they found a peninsula extending into the river and there they built Jamestown. When the Pilgrims completed their explorations of the shores of Cape Cod Bay, they chose the harbor of Plymouth as the best situation for their colony. Lord Baltimore established the Maryland colony at St. Mary's on an arm of the Chesapeake Bay. The Dutch founded New Amsterdam on the island of Manhattan, at the mouth of the Hudson River. The first settlements in each of the colonies were made on the shores of the Atlantic Ocean, or but a few miles up large rivers. Why? The colonists had come to this new world in European vessels which could only bring them to the shore. Here they chose the most convenient place and built their town.

Thus these settlers were in the very beginning familiar with travel by water. But what a poor, inconvenient means of travel it was! The Jamestown colonists, one hundred and five in number, were tossed upon the stormy ocean for more than four months, enduring all the hardships of a severe winter in vessels that to-day would seldom venture upon the ocean, even in coastwise trade. Compare the two months and more of life on the *Mayflower*, where the passengers were crowded into the closest quarters, with the short six or seven days' trip to or from England to-day on the ocean steamers, where travelers find comforts and conveniences almost greater than those they are accustomed to at home.

Although the emigrants suffered greatly in these voyages across the Atlantic Ocean, the day of the return of the vessels to England was a sad one. When the last glimpse of the receding ship had vanished, the homesick watchers realized as never before their isolation—their separation from everybody and everything in which they were interested. Until vessels should again arrive from across the ocean they would be thrown entirely upon their own resources. The settlers were thus very dependent upon the ships that crossed the Atlantic so infrequently and with such difficulty.

Soon after the settlement, however, some of the colonies began to build vessels of their own. The forests provided lumber in great quantity and of the best quality. The first vessel to be built by the Massachusetts Bay Colony was launched at Medford the next year after the settlement of Boston. This small vessel was owned by Governor Winthrop and was appropriately called the *Blessing of the Bay*. The same year a Dutch ship, twenty times as large, was constructed at New Amsterdam.

PILGRIM EXILES.

A large part of the colonial shipbuilding was confined to New England, the *Blessing of the Bay* being but a leader in a long line. Within two years a ship as large as the *Mayflower* was built at Boston, and another twice as large at Salem. Within thirty-five years Boston had one hundred and thirty sail on the sea. New York built fewer but larger ships. Philadelphia was a leading shipbuilding town, and many vessels were constructed in the Carolinas.

The activity of the colonists in thus providing means for travel by water was not limited to ocean shipbuilding. The rivers, the inland roads, already prepared by nature, were used from the very beginning. As the settlements grew, both in population and in numbers, travel between them became more and more necessary, and the rivers and streams came more and more into use. The settlers were wise enough to follow the example of the Indians and to make themselves at once familiar with canoes and small boats of every description.

The earliest form of water travel was, perhaps, the raft. It was usually made of floating logs or bundles of brush tied together. To-day, even, rafts of single logs, merely pointed at the ends, are found in Australia, as well as rafts of reeds. On the coast of Peru rafts seventy feet long and twenty feet broad are common,—large enough to use sails as well as paddles.

The next step was to use the single log, made hollow by gradually burning it out or by slowly chipping away pieces with some sharp implement. On the Atlantic coast the most common form of canoe was the dugout, made from the cedar log; and singularly enough the same tree was most frequently used on the shores of the Pacific Ocean, especially near Puget Sound. These Western boats were frequently of great size, some on the Alaskan coast being ninety feet in length and propelled by forty paddles. The Indians had found these dugouts very serviceable, and as the European colonists began to travel over the same rivers and streams they patterned their river craft after those of the red men.

A BIRCH-BARK CANOE.

The lighter form of the canoe was preferred, where serviceable, to the dugout. This was made of a light but strong framework covered by bark or skins. That used by the Esquimaux was of sealskin stretched over whalebone. But the more common form was the Indian birch-bark canoe, which rapidly became very popular among the colonial hunters and trappers. No better description of the birch canoe can be found than that which the children's poet, Longfellow, gives in "Hiawatha."

> "'Give me of your bark, O Birch Tree!
> Of your yellow bark, O Birch Tree!
> Growing by the rushing river,
> Tall and stately in the valley!
> I a light canoe will build me,
> Build a swift Cheemaun for sailing,
> That shall float upon the river,
> Like a yellow leaf in Autumn,
> Like a yellow water-lily!
>
> "'Lay aside your cloak, O Birch Tree!
> Lay aside your white-skin wrapper,
> For the Summer-time is coming,
> And the sun is warm in heaven,
> And you need no white-skin wrapper!'
>
> "With his knife the tree he girdled;
> Just beneath its lowest branches,
> Just above the roots, he cut it,
> Till the sap came oozing outward;
> Down the trunk, from top to bottom,
> Sheer he cleft the bark asunder,
> With a wooden wedge he raised it,
> Stripped it from the trunk unbroken.

"'Give me of your boughs, O Cedar!
Of your strong and pliant branches,
My canoe to make more steady,
Make more strong and firm beneath me!'

"Down he hewed the boughs of cedar,
Shaped them straightway to a framework,
Like two bows he formed and shaped them,
Like two bended bows together.

"'Give me of your roots, O Tamarack!
Of your fibrous roots, O Larch Tree!
My canoe to bind together,
So to bind the ends together
That the water may not enter,
That the river may not wet me!'

"From the earth he tore the fibres,
Tore the rough roots of the Larch Tree,
Closely sewed the bark together,
Bound it closely to the framework.

"'Give me of your balm, O Fir Tree.
Of your balsam and your resin,
So to close the seams together
That the water may not enter,
That the river may not wet me!'

"And he took the tears of balsam,
Took the resin of the fir tree,
Smeared therewith each seam and fissure,
Made each crevice safe from water.

"Thus the Birch Canoe was builded
In the valley, by the river,
In the bosom of the forest;
And the forest's life was in it,
All its mystery and its magic,
All the lightness of the birch tree,
All the toughness of the cedar,
All the Larch's supple sinews;
And it floated on the river
Like a yellow leaf in Autumn,
Like a yellow water-lily."

CHAPTER III.

STAGECOACHES.

Both by land and by water the methods of travel among the early colonists were extremely rude. From the early days of the settlements until the Independence of the United States the improvement was very slow. During the seventeenth century practically all of the long-distance traveling was by water. Schooners made regular trips from New England to Virginia, and smaller sloops or "packets" ran to New York from the different towns to the eastward. These vessels were dependent, of course, upon the wind, and the length of the journey varied greatly. Perhaps a packet might sail from New Haven to New York in two days, but calms or contrary winds might delay the trip, and make it a week in going from port to port.

On land, however, the facilities for travel slowly but surely improved. An interesting account of the rudeness and hardships of New England land journeys is furnished by the journal of Sarah Knight, who went from Boston to New York on horseback nearly two hundred years ago. The roads were openings in the forest, made by cutting down trees, and were often blocked by fallen trunks. The streams that must be crossed caused the most trouble. "We came," she wrote, "to a river which they generally ride thro'; but I dare not venture; so the post got a ladd and cannoo to carry me to t'other side, and he rid thro' and led my hors. The cannoo was very small and shallow, so that when we were in she seemed ready to take in water, which greatly terrified mee and caused mee to be very circumspect, sitting with my hands fast on each side, my eyes stedy, not daring so much as to lodg my tongue a hair's breadth more on one side of my mouth than t'other, nor so much as think on Lott's wife, for a wry thought would have oversett our wherey." For a woman to undertake such a journey was very unusual, and after her return she wrote with a diamond on the glass of a window these lines:

> "Through many toils and many frights,
> I have returned, poor Sarah Knights.
> Over great rocks and many stones
> God has preserved from fractured bones."

About the time that this long journey was made, carriages began to come into use. The most common of these were the large coach, the "calash," and a lighter, two-wheeled vehicle, with a calash top, similar to a chaise. But these carriages were for a time only used within the towns themselves, where the large number of houses required the building of better roads and streets. Comparatively few persons could afford to own private carriages, and their use was therefore not general for many years. Before the middle of the eighteenth century, however, carriages became more common. Broader and better roads had been built, and longer journeys could be made. As early as 1725, carriages had been driven from the Connecticut River to Boston, and overland travel began to be more customary.

The first roads that could be called suitable for carriage travel were for the most part toll roads. Instead of being made by the towns or counties, or by the colonies, they were built by corporations. These companies were granted the privilege of charging toll from every traveler over their roads for the purpose of paying a profit to the members of the company, as well as to keep the roads in repair. In the same way corporations built bridges, charging a small toll upon every one who crossed them. Thus travel was improved, time was saved, and less discomfort was caused the travelers.

OLD-STYLE CALASHES.

In the eighteenth century public carriages began to come into use. Previously if any one wished to travel by land, he found it necessary to own or hire horses. If he made a voyage by sea, he could pay his fare on some vessel that made the trip he wished to take. This means of public transportation, this carrying a person or his goods for pay, had been limited, however, to water travel. There were no regular conveyances running from town to town by land which would carry passengers or freight.

The town of Plymouth had been settled nearly a hundred years before the first line of stagecoaches in any part of the country was put in operation. This "stage wagon" ran between Boston and Bristol ferry, where it connected with the packet line to Newport and New York. Three years later a stage line began to run from Boston to Newport, making one trip each way every week. The driver advertised to carry "bundles of goods, merchandise, books, men, women, and children."

Travel was slow, much slower than seems possible to-day. The roads were still very poor, in fact scarcely fit to be called roads. Little by little new stage lines were established, nearly always in connection with some packet line. Up to the middle of the eighteenth century, however, opportunities to travel by stage were few and the time required great. Three weeks were needed to make the trip from Boston to Philadelphia, even under the most favorable conditions.

Less than three years before the battle of Lexington, the first stage was run between New York and Boston. The first trip was begun on Monday, July 13th, and the journey's end was not reached until Saturday, July 25th. Thirteen days were thus required for a trip which may now be made in five or six hours. As the amount of travel increased new lines were formed, the roads were improved, and stages were run more frequently and more rapidly. Sixty years after the first trip was made between New York and Boston the time had been cut down from thirteen days to one day and five hours; more than a hundred lines of coaches were then regularly running out of Boston.

In spite, however, of every improvement, travel by stage a hundred years ago was no simple or pleasant matter. Professor McMaster says: "The stagecoach was little better than a huge covered box mounted on springs. It had neither glass windows nor door nor steps nor closed sides. The roof was upheld by eight posts which rose from the body of the vehicle, and the body was commonly breast-high. From the top were hung curtains of leather, to be drawn up when the day was fine and let down and buttoned when rainy or cold. Within were four seats. Without was the baggage. When the baggage had all been weighed and strapped on the coach, when the horses had been attached, the eleven passengers were summoned, and, clambering to their seats through the front of the stage, sat down with their faces toward the driver's seat."

AN OLD-FASHIONED STAGECOACH.

The coach would set out from the inn with the horses on a gallop, which would continue until a steep hill was reached. Then would follow the slow pacing up the hill, the gallop down again, the dragging through a stretch of muddy road, the careful fording of a river, the watering of the horses every few miles, and the rapid gallop up to the next inn. Here the mail pouches would be taken out and in, perhaps a change of coaches made or more frequently of horses only, a delay for a little gossip, and the stage would be off again. This was all very exhilarating and agreeable in pleasant, warm weather, but how fatiguing in the cold and snows of winter, and even during a chilly summer storm.

These public conveyances were used only when necessary. Private carriages were much preferred to the stagecoach, as being a more comfortable as well as a safer mode of travel. The story is told of one young lady who was visiting near Boston, eighty years ago. She was very anxious to return to her home, but her father was unable to come for her. Her mother wrote: "Your papa would not trust your life in the stage. It is a very unsafe and improper conveyance for young ladies. Many have been the accidents, many the cripples made by accidents in these vehicles. As soon as your papa can, you may be sure he will go or send for you."

MUNROE TAVERN, LEXINGTON, MASS. (BUILT IN 1695.)

Whether the traveler went by stage or in his private carriage, it was necessary to stop at the inns. The taverns had a great deal to do with making journeys pleasant or disagreeable. As a general rule, the New England inns were kept by leading men, and in most cases the innkeeper was required to obtain recommendations from the selectmen of the town before he could get a license or a permission to establish and keep the tavern. Even the smaller New England villages boasted of inns that compared favorably with the hotels of the large towns. A Frenchman, traveling through the United States early in this century, wrote in highest praise of the inns of New England, whose windows were without shutters, and whose doors had neither locks nor keys, and yet where no harm ever came to the traveler. He admired "the great room, with its low ceiling and neatly sanded floor; its bright pewter dishes and stout-backed, slat-bottomed chairs ranged along its walls; its long table; and its huge fireplace, with the benches on either side."

He had less praise for the inns of the rest of the country. The buildings were poor, the fare was coarse, and the beds were bad. The roofs leaked, the windows were sometimes mere openings in the wall; the bedding was unclean and extremely uninviting.

If a traveler were compelled to stop at the Southern inns, he found his journey far from agreeable. Fortunately for him the Southern planter was the most hospitable of persons. "At his home strangers were heartily welcome and nobly entertained. Some bade their slaves ask in any traveler that might be seen passing by. Some kept servants on the watch to give notice of every approaching horseman or of the distant rumble of a coming coach and four." On the plantation the traveler was always treated as a most intimate friend, and in the cheery comfort of the mansion he forgot, for the time being, the trials and hardships of travel by land.

CHAPTER IV.

STEAMBOATS.

The idea of payment for transportation is very old. Thousands of years ago we read of vessels sailing upon the Mediterranean Sea prepared to transport persons or freight for sums of money. Where this idea originated is not known, but it may have occurred to a savage for the first time in some such way as the following:

A hunter lived on the banks of a river in Asia. One day he shot a duck which fell to the ground on the opposite shore. The hunter needed the bird, for he was hungry, but how was he to obtain it? The river was very deep at this point, and he could not swim. He knew that there was a shallow place five miles up the stream, where he might ford the river, and another ford five miles below. But to cross by either of these would require a journey of ten miles to the bird and ten miles back, just to get across a narrow river. He remembered that a big log lay upon a sand-bar in the river not far from where he was. He took a pole, pried off the log and rolled it into the water. Then seating himself on it he poled himself across, obtained the duck, and soon reached his home again. Here was the first water travel.

A few days later he heard a cry from over the river. Looking up, he saw a man who desired to cross. The stranger called to him to get his log and take him over, as he had carried himself. The hunter saw that the stranger had a deer on his shoulder. He was hungry, and therefore called out: "Give me the hind leg and half the loin of your deer for my labor, and I will bring you safely over." The stranger promptly agreed, and the hunter poled across the river. In some such way doubtless was the first payment made for transportation, and the idea soon became common that it was just and proper to charge a fare for carrying freight and passengers.

What powers have we found used in transportation up to a hundred years ago? First there was human power, either walking or plying oars or paddles. This energy is limited; walking is necessarily a slow process, and rowing is seldom a rapid mode of travel. Then came horse power, used first to carry travelers or goods and later to draw carriages and wagons, conveying passengers and freight. Horse power is superior to human power both in speed and in endurance, but it also has its limits and often fails at important times.

Then use was made of the wind, which, blowing against stretches of canvas, propelled vessels. Here was no human power to become wearied; no horse power to fail at the wrong time. Vessels need not stop at night in order to sleep, nor even at noon in order to take dinner. But the wind is fickle; it does not always blow;

it frequently blows from the wrong direction; it often blows too much. Human power, horse power, wind power, each was insufficient or unsatisfactory, and the time was ripe for some power stronger and less fickle to produce more rapid transportation.

When the necessity of a new power became great, the needed energy and a way to use it were soon found. Near the close of the eighteenth century a number of men, unacquainted with each other's ideas, began to experiment with steam as a means for propelling vessels. Why had they not begun earlier? For two reasons. The demand for quicker water travel had but just commenced, and the fact that steam could practically be used as a motive power was only beginning to be understood.

It so happened that James Watt's steam engine was perfected just as the treaty of peace with Great Britain acknowledged the independence of the United States. Now American inventors were able to make use of the steam engine to aid travel and transportation. At once they began work. Samuel Morey built a steamboat on the upper Connecticut River; James Rumsey experimented on the Potomac; John Fitch on the Delaware, and William Longstreet on the Savannah; Oliver Evans was at work in Philadelphia, and John Stevens on the Hudson.

FITCH'S STEAMBOAT.

One of these boats used the steam engine to move oars; another pumped water in at the bow and forced it out again at the stern; a third had a wheel in the stern; and a fourth had a paddle wheel on each side. Some of the vessels used upright, and some horizontal engines. Most of these inventors succeeded in running their boats against the tide or the current of rivers, and proved that steam could be thus used. Each may be said to have invented a steamboat. But these men were all without means; they did not succeed in awakening the interest of wealthy men; and the public cared little about such inventions. Therefore each of these steamboats was given up in turn and soon forgotten; the eighteenth century passed away, and no practical result had appeared. It is natural to have more interest in the account of an invention which proved of practical value than in the stories of even successful attempts which were given up almost as soon as made.

Robert Fulton was born in Pennsylvania just as Watt began his study of the steam engine. Almost as soon as Watt had completed his improvements on the engine, Fulton came of age, and went to England to study painting with Benjamin West, the famous American artist. In the midst of his art studies he became interested in mechanical pursuits. He attracted the attention of some English scientists, and, by their encouragement, he abandoned painting and devoted himself to inventing. But who knows how much assistance his skill in drawing may have been to him in his preparations of plans and models?

Joel Barlow, a noted American poet, was then living in France, and upon his invitation Fulton spent several years in his home in Paris. Here he devoted his time to boats, as he had already done in London. His schemes were of various kinds. He planned diving boats, steamboats, and canal boats, and was particularly interested in a boat which he called a marine torpedo. This boat he planned to be used to injure vessels in naval warfare. For a time he neglected the steamboat, and bent every energy to persuade the French Government to adopt the torpedo. Afterward he urged his marine boats upon the English and American governments, but in vain. He did not realize the enormously greater future value of the steamboat.

In time, however, Fulton finished his plans, and a steamboat was built for him upon the river Seine. The next step was to enlist the coöperation of some one with power and means by proving that the invention was valuable. Fulton accordingly sought to bring the boat to the attention of the French Emperor. He succeeded in awakening Napoleon's interest. It was just at the time that the emperor was planning to take his great army across the Channel to attack England. He saw that steamboats, if of practical value, would be serviceable to him in these plans. Accordingly he directed a scientific committee to attend a public trial of the boat.

A day was set for the examination. Fulton had worked steadily for weeks, seeking to make every part as perfect as possible. The night before the appointed day, Fulton retired for rest, but sleep would not come to his eyes. His thoughts were so completely fixed upon his invention and what the next day meant to him that he could not control them. Not until morning began to dawn did he catch a nap, and then only to be immediately awakened by a knock at his door.

A messenger had come to tell him that his boat was at the bottom of the river.

The iron machinery had proved too heavy for the little sixteen-foot boat, and had broken through. Fulton's hopes were at an end. Before he could build another boat and make another engine the opportunity would be past. His disappointment was intense. However, he did not despair, but was soon ready to try again.

Doubtless the failure was a blessing in disguise. The boat was probably too small to make a successful trip. The next time he would have a larger vessel. Instead of again trying to arouse French interest, he decided to make the next experiment at home.

Robert R. Livingston, our minister to France, who together with James Monroe purchased for the United States the great province of Louisiana, had long been interested in the possibilities of steam navigation. He entered into Fulton's plans and assisted him in every way. Soon after the disaster on the Seine both men returned to America, and the next six months were spent in building a boat and in putting into it a steam engine which they had especially ordered in Birmingham, England. A grant had been obtained from the New York legislature which gave them the exclusive right to run steam vessels on any of the waters of the State.

The new boat was a hundred and thirty feet in length, or eight times as long as that lost in the Seine. It was called the *Clermont*, after the country home of Livingston. It was a side-paddle steamboat, with wheels fifteen feet in diameter and four feet wide. The trial trip was announced for August 7th, 1807, and at one o'clock in the afternoon the *Clermont* stood at the wharf in New York ready for the journey.

Was the trial to succeed or fail? To succeed, the *Clermont* must steam up the Hudson River at a speed of, at least, four miles an hour. The trip proposed was from New York to Albany, a distance of one hundred and fifty miles, and return. This trip was regularly made by sailing packets, and the average time was four days. Could the *Clermont* reach Albany in thirty-seven hours, or a day and a half? Unfortunately, a north wind was blowing, which would greatly decrease the speed.

Fulton and Livingston were confident that it could be done. The steamboat left the wharf and slowly sailed up the river. Soon the faults natural to a new invention began to show themselves. The rudder did not work as it ought; the wheels were unprotected by a covering; the vessel sank too far in the water. But the trial, in spite of all the odds against it, was successful. The one hundred and fifty miles were made in thirty-two hours, with five hours to spare from the limit set. If we subtract the time spent in stops, but twenty-eight and a half hours were used, making an average of more than five miles an hour.

The first long steamboat trip had been accomplished. The indifference of the public at once changed to enthusiasm. Fulton was immediately urged to make regular trips, and, although the *Clermont* needed many improvements, he consented. The next winter, however, the boat was removed from the river for repairs; but in the spring regular trips were resumed, and the steamboat became a new and permanent means of transportation.

There was abundant opportunity to improve the steamboat and develop its use. At first Fulton's *Clermont* alone steamed up and down the Hudson River.

Soon, however, other steamboats were built to run in opposition to the sailing packets. Steamers began to ply on Lake Champlain and on the Delaware River. Three years after the first voyage of the *Clermont*, a steamboat was making three trips a week from New York to New Brunswick, New Jersey; here the traveler took stage for Bordentown on the Delaware River, whence another boat carried him to Philadelphia. Two years later steam ferryboats ran between New York and the Jersey shore.

The first river steamboat was launched at Pittsburg, and was sent down the Ohio and the Mississippi to New Orleans in 1811. Three years later the *Ætna* steamed from Pittsburg to New Orleans, and back to Louisville. The same year a steamboat was built on the Lakes to run from Buffalo to Detroit, and a company was organized to start a steamship line from New York to Charleston. Five years afterward the steamship *Savannah*, using both steam and sails, crossed the Atlantic Ocean. She made but slow time, and the great space required to hold the fuel left little room for freight. Year by year, however, improvements were made on the vessels and quicker time was the result. Finally, anthracite coal came into general use, and thirty years after the trial trip of the *Clermont*, the steamers *Sirius* and the *Great Western* began regular trips between Liverpool and New York. The day of steam navigation had come, and from that time on the vexatious delays due to fickle winds no longer need be a cause of trouble.

CHAPTER V.

CANALS.

NINETY years ago, two brothers, James and John, found it necessary to make the long journey from their home in New York City to Kentucky. They had frequently traveled through the country, and were familiar with stages and packets. This time they proposed to make their first trip on the steamboat, since the *Clermont* was again making its regular runs. It was advertised to leave New York at one o'clock on Wednesday. The brothers felt no need of haste in their preparations for the journey, and it was nearly two o'clock before they came in sight of the wharf. Just then John made the remark that they were very foolish to arrive so early.

"We shall have to wait an hour or two," he said; "the boat won't be ready to start before three o'clock at the earliest."

"I am not so sure," was the reply. "Perhaps the steamboat will not be as late as the packets."

When they reached the wharf, no steamboat was there. Far up the river they saw, slowly moving off in the distance, a vessel, which they knew must be the *Clermont*, from the line of smoke that lay behind it. Immediately they began to inquire what it meant and were told, "Oh! that is one of Fulton's notions. He has given strict orders that the boat shall always leave the wharf exactly on advertised time." This was a novelty almost as great as the steamboat itself. Sailing vessels had been dependent upon the wind, and stages upon the conditions of the roads and the weather; neither made any pretence of running upon schedule time. Fulton's idea of punctuality was new and caused much grumbling for a time; but with the coming of the railroads it became an absolute necessity.

What were the two men to do? But two things could be done. They might take passage on a packet, or wait for the next trip of the *Clermont*. They decided to wait, as they were anxious to try the steamboat; they had had enough experience with the slow sailing vessels, and their poor accommodations. They did not permit themselves to be late a second time. In fact, the clocks had hardly struck twelve when they stepped aboard the *Clermont*.

The hour before the departure of the boat was spent in examining it from stem to stern. The original *Clermont* had been greatly improved. The wheels were now properly protected; a rudder, specially adapted to the boat and the river, had been constructed. Most noticeable were the accommodations for the passengers, which were almost elegant when compared with the poor quarters of the packets. In fact the *Clermont* had become "a floating palace, gay with ornamental painting, gilding, and polished woods."

At one o'clock sharp the boat quietly left the wharf. The wind was blowing freshly down the river and the tide was going out. A packet started at the same moment from a neighboring pier. The steamboat at once turned its prow up the stream, but the packet headed for the Jersey shore, as it could sail against the wind only by making long tacks. This greatly increased the distance it had to travel, and before sunset the *Clermont* had left the packet many miles behind.

The next morning everything was still going smoothly when the two passengers saw a little way ahead another packet, which had left New York before the steamboat. This sloop was making tacks like those they had watched the previous afternoon, and the *Clermont* was rapidly gaining on it. Suddenly John exclaimed, "What are they doing? Are they trying to run us down?" It was evident that the packet was coming straight for the steamboat; but the captain of the *Clermont* shut off steam at once and the packet passed its bow without doing harm.

COLLISION OF THE CLERMONT AND THE SLOOP.

Soon a sloop was met coming down the river. Again came the exclamation from John, "They are surely trying to run into us!" He had hardly spoken when the crash came; the packet struck the wheel box, tore it open, and then, sliding along the side of the steamboat, passed away down the river. On inquiry John ascertained that this was merely an illustration of the envy of the owners of packets, who feared that they would lose all their business. No serious damage was done, however, and the steamboat proceeded on its way.

The *Clermont* arrived at Albany at seven o'clock Thursday evening and the brothers spent the night at an inn. The next morning, after an early breakfast, a stage was taken which in a few hours carried them to Schenectady. This part of the journey was quickly made, as the road was one of the best in the country. On reaching Schenectady the travelers learned that they must wait till the next noon to take a boat up the Mohawk River. The hours slowly dragged along, another night was spent at an inn, and about three o'clock the next afternoon the slow trip up the Mohawk began. Two days later they reached Utica, and another stage took them, the next day, to Rome. From this village two days' sail carried them across the Oneida Lake, and down the Oswego River to Oswego on the banks of Lake Ontario.

After a delay of thirty-six hours a lake packet was found ready for them, which in time arrived at Lewiston at the mouth of the Niagara River, and so on they went, by land to Buffalo, by water to Erie, by land again to one of the branches of the Alleghany River, and down this to Pittsburg. From Pittsburg one of the flat-bottomed Western river boats, borne along by the current, conveyed them to Louisville, at the Falls of the Ohio.

Thus was made, in several weeks, a trip from New York to Louisville, which to-day requires scarcely more than twenty-four hours. Ten times had changes been made in the conveyances used. A steamboat, river rowboats, lake packets, Western flatboats and stages, were all needed, and nights and days even were spent at inns. Slow and cumbrous was travel in those days and very expensive. There was little traveling for pleasure, and only the most important business was worth the hardships and discomforts of such travel.

If it was costly for passengers to travel, it was even more expensive to carry freight. Enormous charges were placed upon all transportation of goods. New and better roads were being built in all directions, but these did little to reduce the cost of transporting goods. The cheapest routes continued to be by the rivers, as the expense of building good roads and keeping them in repair added to freight charges. The charges for freight transportation were so great that it prevented entirely the moving of many goods.

The people in Pennsylvania desired the salt which was obtained in New York, but it cost $2.50 a bushel to carry salt three hundred miles. Citizens of Philadelphia would have purchased flour which was raised about the sources of the Susquehanna River had it not cost $1.50 a barrel to carry it to Philadelphia. Hundreds of families were weekly moving westward into the new country across the Alleghany Mountains; they could not afford to take their household goods with them. The freight charges from New York to Buffalo were $120 a ton; from Philadelphia to Pittsburg, $125.

Something new in the line of transportation was needed; some way by which freight could be carried at less expense. Private companies were building new toll roads—but these did not accomplish the purpose. Different States expended money in improving the highways, and still the expense of transportation was enormous. The national Government also took part in the work and constructed a highway from Cumberland, Maryland, to Wheeling, on the Ohio River—but this was merely a single road over the mountains, and freight charges were as high as ever.

What could be done? Of course the roads everywhere must be improved and new ones built—all of which would take many years. But was there not some way to avoid carrying so much freight in wagons drawn by horses? Wherever there were rivers these could be used. Was it possible to make rivers, or at least to make water-ways, upon which boats might be used? The people of the United States began to talk of canals, and soon enthusiasm for canal building became universal.

What is a canal? It is a trench cut in the ground, filled with water deep enough for a well-laden boat, and wide enough for boats to pass each other. On one bank is a path, called the towpath, upon which horses or mules travel, pulling a canal boat behind them by means of a long rope. In most canals it is found necessary to lift the boats over higher land or up to a higher level. This is done by locks, which are built where the two levels of the canal come together. These locks are shut off from each part of the canal by gates. When the lower gates are shut and the upper gates open, water is let into the lock from the upper canal until on a level with it. Then a canal boat from the upper canal enters the lock. The upper gates are closed, the lower gates opened, and the water runs out of the lock. The boat, remaining on top of the water, sinks to the lower level and is ready to proceed on its course. In traveling the other way the process is turned about. The boat enters the lock and rises with the water which is let in from above until it is on the upper level.

Canals, with their locks, are simple and easily built. The expense lies mainly in digging the trench. When the canal is once finished the cost of running is very slight, and freight can be carried much more cheaply than over roads, or even by the natural rivers. Canal travel is very slow, however, as the boat is drawn by a horse at a slow walk. Therefore a canal is used, for the most part, to carry freight, especially freight not very perishable. Garden vegetables, fruit, and meats, for example, are not carried on canals to any great distance; on the other hand, the length of time used in conveying salt, or flour, or household goods, is not of so much importance.

Plans for canals sprang up all at once throughout the country. The Middlesex canal in Massachusetts and the Blackstone canal between Providence and Worcester were among the first built. The Delaware and Hudson canal in New York, and the Chesapeake and Delaware in Maryland were of early importance. In time nearly every Atlantic State had one or more canals as aids to transportation. Many of them were of additional importance because they connected neighboring bays, and could furnish opportunities for water travel, even when the harbors might be blockaded in time of war.

The greatest and by far the most important is the Erie canal, which connects Buffalo on Lake Erie with Albany on the Hudson River. This canal was due to the energy and persistence of Governor De Witt Clinton, who dug the first shovelful of earth in 1817, and made the first trip over the completed canal in 1825. There was great opposition to building this canal at the expense of the State, and the nickname of "Clinton's Big Ditch" was frequently applied to it.

Governor Clinton was wiser, however, than his opponents. Every cent spent on this canal, which is 363 miles long, 40 feet wide, and 4 feet deep, was wisely spent. On the day that it was finished the great prosperity of New York City began. A large part of the trade and commerce between the East and the West was carried over the Erie canal, because it furnished the cheapest route. Freight charges between Buffalo and Albany fell at once to less than one-quarter their former rates, and continued to decrease until they became less than $10 a ton.

THE ERIE CANAL.

Thus far had travel and transportation improved. From walking, horseback riding, and rowboats, slow changes had led to stages, packets, steamboats, and canals. From the simple Indian trail, like the Bay Path, had grown up the great highways, like the National Road. From slow and difficult journeys between neighboring towns, traveling had become easy from Maine to Florida, and from the Atlantic Ocean to the Mississippi River. Was there any chance for further improvement?

CHAPTER VI.

RAILROADS.

Up to this time progress had been more marked upon the water than upon the land. On the land travelers were still limited to human power and horse power. On the water, however, not only human power and wind were used, but also horse power and even steam power. The steamboat was thought to be the most rapid means of transit possible. No energy was known greater than that of steam; therefore no new source of power was expected.

If steam could aid water navigation, could it not be used in land travel? This question was ever present in the minds of inventors, mechanics, and travelers on both sides of the ocean. Little by little an answer was obtained, and the field of steam was enlarged. Even before Fulton's trial trip, the first step in the direction of the railroad was taken, though steam had nothing to do with this first practical experiment.

The city of Boston was built upon three hills, two of which have now been almost entirely moved away. Upon the third, called Beacon Hill, was built the State House. Early in this century the top of this hill was lowered by carrying away the gravel. For this purpose a tramway was built. This consisted of two sets of rails or tracks from the top to the bottom of the hill, upon which cars were used. The full car on one track ran down of its own weight, pulling up the empty car on the other track. This was the first use of rails in this country.

The first permanent tramway was built in Pennsylvania. Thomas Leifer owned a stone quarry about three-quarters of a mile from the nearest wharf on the Delaware River. He desired to carry his stone to tide water more easily than by the ordinary methods. Accordingly he built a tramway from the quarry to the wharf, and placed upon the tracks an ordinary wagon. To this he attached horses and had what we should call a horse car. The rails made a smooth road over which his horses could draw five tons as easily as one ton over the common roads. This tram was used regularly for eighteen years.

One-half of the steam railroad had now been invented. The tramway was the railroad—now steam must be applied. That was all. But that was not so easy as it would seem now. Year after year passed and no one attempted it. Doubtless many persons felt certain that the steam railroads were coming some time and that they would be of value, just as to-day many people expect that travel through the air is coming some time. At the same time there were many who did not believe that steam could be used for land travel at all; while others did not care to have it come for fear that travel would be made too speedy.

One of the leading English magazines took occasion to express its opinion concerning a proposed railway: "What can be more absurd and ridiculous than the prospect held out of locomotives traveling *twice as fast as stage coaches*! We should as soon expect the people of Woolwich to suffer themselves to be fired off upon one of Congreve's rockets as trust themselves to the mercy of a machine going at such a rate. We trust that Parliament will, in all railways it may sanction, limit the speed to *eight or nine miles an hour*, which is as great as can be ventured on with safety." What would this writer say to the safety of the trains of to-day, as they make forty fifty, sixty, and even seventy miles an hour?

Many of the inventions which have done the most for mankind have been made by Americans, but we owe the locomotive to an Englishman. George Stephenson from early boyhood devoted himself to the study of engines and machinery. When but thirteen years of age he assisted his father in the care of an engine at a coal mine near Newcastle. Working by day as an engineman, and studying by night in a night school, he prepared himself for his future work. He won the confidence of his employers, especially that of Lord Ravensworth, who supplied him with funds to build a "traveling engine" to run on the rails of the tramroad between the mines and the shipping port, nine miles distant. July 25th, 1814, Stephenson made a successful trip with his locomotive, "My Lord," which pulled the coal cars at the rate of four miles an hour.

Stephenson felt that this locomotive was but a beginning. He told his friends that "there was no limit to the speed of such an engine, if the works could be made to stand." He was still pursuing his studies and experiments when he was appointed engineer of a proposed railroad between Stockton and Darlington. The directors of the road had planned to pull their cars by horses, but they were won over by Stephenson to agree to try an engine. Eleven years after the trial trip of his first engine, Stephenson was ready to exhibit a locomotive upon a railroad joining two towns for the purpose of transporting passengers and freight.

A short time before the trial trip, Stephenson made a prediction concerning the future of his invention. "I venture to tell you," he said, "that I think that you will live to see the day when railways will supersede almost all other methods of conveyance in this country—when mail coaches will go by railway, and railroads will become the great highways for the king and all his subjects. The time is coming when it will be cheaper for a working man to travel on a railway than to walk on foot. I know that there are great and almost insurmountable difficulties to be encountered, but what I have said will come to pass as sure as you now hear me."

The Stockton and Darlington Railway was three years in process of construction, and the day of its opening, September 27th, 1825, was an important one in the history of travel. Imagine that first train load—the locomotive, guided by Stephenson himself, six freight cars, a car carrying "distinguished guests," twenty-one coal cars crammed with passengers, and six more freight cars all loaded. Ahead of the train, or procession, as it might be called, rode a man on horseback, carrying a flag bearing the motto, "The private risk is the public benefit." When the train started, crowds of people ran along by its side, for a time easily keeping up with it. Finally, however, Stephenson called to the horseman to get out of the way and, putting on steam, drove the engine at the rate of fifteen miles an hour. The future of the locomotive was assured.

Americans were ready for new methods of traveling. Three years after the opening of the first passenger steam-railway in England, the Baltimore and Ohio Railroad began to construct a line from Baltimore westward, and in two years fourteen miles were opened to travel. For a year, however, horses were used as motive power; in 1831, the road advertised for locomotives. Meanwhile an engine, called the "Stombridge Lion," was brought over from England, in 1829, and used on a line built by the Delaware and Hudson Canal Company. It was found to be too heavy and was abandoned. The second locomotive used in this country, "The Best Friend of Charleston," was built in New York City, and was run on the South Carolina Railroad.

OLD-STYLE RAILROAD TRAIN.

The locomotive and the railroad had come, such as they were. The locomotive had its boiler and its smokestack, its cylinders and driving wheels; but it had no cab for the engineer and the fireman, and no brake to stop the train. The tender was but a flat car, carrying fuel and water. The cars were merely stagecoaches made to run on rails, and in no way were the passengers protected from the smoke and cinders of the burning wood. Yet this poor, inconvenient railroad was a great advance in itself, and it foretold greater advances in the days to come.

In 1835, five years after the opening of the first steam railroad in the United States, there were twenty-three roads and over a thousand miles of track. After 1835, an average of nearly four hundred miles was built yearly until 1848. From that time until the beginning of the Civil War, railroad construction proceeded with great rapidity, nearly two thousand miles of railroad being built each year. In 1849, a continuous line of railroad was completed between New York and Boston. Two years later two distinct lines were finished, connecting New York and Buffalo. At the end of another two years, through connection was had between New York and Chicago. At the same time railroads were being built in all sections east of the Mississippi River.

After peace was restored in 1865, came a great period of railroad building. During ten years the number of miles of railroad more than doubled, nearly four thousand miles being built each year. This was the period when the continuous lines, which had already reached the Missouri River, were continued across the continent. After five years of labor the Union Pacific Railroad, starting at Omaha, Nebraska, met at Ogden, Utah, the Central Pacific, which had been built from Sacramento, California. May 10th, 1869, the last spike was driven and the Pacific coast was bound to the Atlantic by bands of steel.

Since the completion of the Union and Central Pacific railroads, four other through lines have been constructed across the Rocky Mountains, within the territory of the United States, and one in Canada. It is now possible to go from ocean to ocean in less than five days, and to have such a choice of routes that neither the cold of winter nor the heat of summer need be troublesome.

At last the limit of rapid traveling seems to have been reached. Walking and horseback riding are indulged in only for pleasure and health; stagecoaches are used only for short lines where the railroad has not yet come; but all the long-distance traveling is now done behind the locomotive. Journeys of weeks have become trips of a few days, days have been lessened to hours, and the country has become knit together by rapid transit. Is there a chance for further improvement?

CHAPTER VII.

MODERN WATER TRAVEL.

James Greenleaf arrived in Duluth, one bright June day, four hundred and five years after the discovery of America. For nearly forty years he had been a missionary among the Indians of the British Northwest, but he had finally been persuaded to take a well-earned rest. Leaving his little settlement of red men, and taking a canoe, he had paddled up stream, carried his canoe over a portage, and paddled down a river until he reached Lake Superior, where a small sailboat had taken him to the flourishing city at the western end of the lake.

At the hotel he found, as he expected, his nephew, Henry Towne. Mr. Towne was a commercial traveler, always "on the road," as he would say, for a large furniture establishment in New York. In a letter to his uncle he had stated that business would call him to Minnesota at just that time, and that he would make the journey with his uncle from Duluth to New York.

The next day the two men started. The nephew had made all the necessary arrangements, having purchased tickets and engaged staterooms on the line of steamboats that connect Duluth with Buffalo. The first sight of the steamboat caused Mr. Greenleaf to exclaim at its size.

"It is not much like the steamboat that I took on the Hudson in the spring of 1856," he said. "I imagine, however, that I shall see greater differences than this, the further I go."

As the two men made a tour through the steamboat, the older gave expression to his thoughts in many ways.

"We did not have the saloon in those old days, when I did my traveling. Whenever we did not care to remain on the open deck there was no parlor to which we could go. No orchestra helped to while away our hours. No piano or organ added the charm of music to our journey."

"But you had a state room to which you could retire," replied his companion, as they came to the rooms numbered 240 and 242, which numbers were on the keys that they had obtained at the purser's.

"Yes," said his uncle, "a tiny room, six feet by six, with narrow little berths, and two small stools. I can assure you that it was nothing like these comfortable sleeping rooms, brilliantly lighted, with regulation beds, convenient toilet arrangements, and carpeted floors. However, I do not imagine that the machinery will let me sleep any better now than then."

The next morning, as the travelers went down to breakfast, the younger man asked, "Well, uncle, how did you sleep?"

"Never better," was the reply. "I tell you, Henry, I want to look at the machinery, after breakfast. It must be somewhat unlike the engine of my day, or the boat, large though it is, would have more of a jar."

When the two men stood above the mammoth engine and noted the smooth working parts, the regular and even motion of the great piston rods in and out of the cylinders, the quietness and gentleness with which each movement took place, the uncle said: "More improvements have been made on the engine of forty years ago than had then been made on that of the *Clermont*. And we used to think that the steamboats of our day were as much superior to Fulton's boat as his was ahead of Fitch's steam-moved paddles."

We cannot take note of all the novel sensations that came to the old missionary, nor can we pause to relate many of the conversations between the two men. We can record a few only of the greater changes which were discussed as they continued their journey, and mention some of the comments called forth by the scenes through which Mr. Greenleaf was passing.

On the afternoon of the second day the steamboat passed through the locks of the canal at Sault Ste. Marie.

"Uncle," remarked the drummer, "how does this canal compare with the Delaware and Hudson canal, with which you were familiar?"

"How can they be compared?" replied his uncle. "That was a long trench, hardly more than a scratch on the surface of the ground. This is broad and deep, though not long."

"Yes," said Mr. Towne, "but there is no new principle here. This canal is somewhat wider and deeper; its locks and gates are somewhat larger. Still it is only a canal."

"But we could not make such a hole in our day. We could not afford to hire men enough to dig it; it must have required many years to make this excavation."

"Oh; this canal was not made as large as this when it was first built. It has been enlarged since. But you know that we do not do all our digging now by hand. Steam shovels do the work for us. That gives us a great advantage over the day laborer with his pick and shovel."

"What strikes me as most noticeable," said Mr. Greenleaf, "is the number of vessels waiting on both sides of the lock. What causes such a crowd to-day, particularly?"

"This is no unusual number," replied Mr. Towne. "You do not realize what a traffic there is on the great lakes. It is stated that the tonnage passing through this canal is greater than that through any other strait on the face of the globe. This growth is very recent and very rapid."

"But what causes the traffic and where are all the vessels going?" asked the missionary.

"The great bulk of the freight," answered the younger man, "is grain from the Northwest, and iron, copper, coal, and lumber, now being obtained in vast quantities south of Lake Superior. So long as the steamboats can carry freight more cheaply than the steam cars, grain and ores will take this route. Sometime we shall have canals large enough for ocean steamers, which will connect the great lakes with the Atlantic Ocean. Then we can load our freight at Chicago or Duluth and not change it until it is unloaded at some English or European port."

The next day, as the steamboat was lying at the wharf at Detroit, conversation was turned to the great ferryboats plying across the river.

"I notice great changes in the steam ferries, since last I crossed the North River at New York," remarked Mr. Greenleaf.

"Yes," was the reply, "but you see only improvements. The ferryboats are larger and you might almost say clumsier; that is all."

"I do not think so," returned the missionary. "There must be some new invention to enable entire trains, with cars filled with passengers, to be carried across such a river as this."

"Of course," said his nephew, "the boat must be strong and large. However, the ferry docks have been improved. Now, when the boat is fastened, the wharf can be raised and lowered, until it is exactly on the level of the boat. Then not only passengers, but wagons and steam cars can pass from one to the other almost without knowledge of the change."

"How far have these cars come that I see on the ferry?"

"That," said the drummer, "is one of the through trains from Montreal to Chicago. The ferryboat next beyond, going the other way, bears a train containing cars bound for New York and Boston."

"Well, well! This is convenient," said the missionary. "The passengers are saved much trouble by not being required to gather up all their traveling bundles, leave the cars for the boat, and the boat for a new set of cars. We should have thought this a great gain, forty years ago."

"But do you realize what an inconvenience this ferry causes? Much time is wasted, not only because of the slow movement of the boats, but also from the necessary delays in embarking and disembarking the cars."

"Yes, I suppose so. But what would you do? Here is the river and it is too wide for a bridge."

"Oh, no!" replied Mr. Towne. "The bridge could be built, but it would be expensive and would not pay. But what do you think of a tunnel?"

"A tunnel? What do you mean?" said the other man, with a touch of surprise in his voice for the first time. "A tunnel? Where? Not under the river?

"Yes," answered his nephew, "a tunnel under the river. There is one, a few miles north, at Port Huron. There the train, instead of being delayed hours by the ferry, passes at almost full speed directly under the river, proceeding on its way as though the river were not there."

"Is not that something new?" asked Mr. Greenleaf.

A RIVER TUNNEL.

"Yes. It was opened only a half-dozen years ago. It is said to be the greatest river tunnel in the world. It is a little over a mile long and is fifteen feet below the bed of the St. Clair River. Half a mile of it is directly under the water, yet no one passing through it would realize that it was different from any one of the hundreds of tunnels through which the railroads of this country pass. It is but a natural following out of such tunnels as the five-mile tunnel under the Hoosac Mountains in Massachusetts, or the three-quarter-mile tunnels in Jersey City, or the score of tunnels on the line of the Southern Railway over the Blue Ridge in North Carolina. It is a great tunnel to-day, of course, but when the North River tunnel is finished, from New York to Jersey City, this will be of little account in comparison."

Detroit was soon left, Lake Erie was reached, and night came on. The next morning the steamboat reached its journey's end at Buffalo. Our friends hastened across the city and were soon seated in a sleeper, on the train for New York.

CHAPTER VIII.

MODERN LAND TRAVEL.

Soon after the train had started from the Buffalo station conversation began between Mr. Greenleaf and his nephew. "The steam is the same as in my day," remarked the former; "the steam pushes the piston in just the same way; there is no change in this direction. But all else is new."

"Yes," said the drummer, "you must see great changes; tell me some of them."

"Very well," was the reply. "The most noticeable thing about a railroad train used to be the jerking motion. We seemed to be going 'bump-i-ty-bump' all the time; and starting and stopping a train would often throw us off our feet."

"Various improvements," said Mr. Towne, "have helped to produce this easy-riding motion. The roadbeds are laid with much greater care—long experience and numerous experiments have provided us with the best rails; but more especially the absence of jar is due to steel springs, and also to the breaks and couplers. When one car was attached to another by two bolts thrust through a ring, nothing was firm, as the bolts would slide forward and back with every motion of the car. The new automatic couplers hold the two cars more firmly together. Again, the old hand brakes have been replaced by the automatic air brake."

"Yes, I have heard of that, but I do not understand it. Can you explain it to me?"

"I think so. George Westinghouse, Jr., about thirty years ago, took out a patent for the air brake. This alone has been enough to make him famous, although he has twelve hundred patents issued in his name. The Westinghouse air brake is now almost universally used. Some of the surplus steam in the locomotive pumps air into tanks in the cars, which air presses upon a piston, that moves a rod against the brakes. Thus the brakes can be held against the wheels with great force at the will of the engineer."

"Well, the next thing that I notice," said the missionary, "is the improved comfort of the passengers. The cinders filled the cars in the old days; the air within was always bad; the candles gave more smoke than light; and in winter, the stoves at the end of the cars gave no heat in the center."

"Yes, all that is changed," replied the younger man. "Spark arresters keep out the cinders; the overhead ventilators give us good air; bright light, almost like that of day, surrounds us in the evening; and, when wanted, the engine supplies steam in pipes running the entire length of the car, which gives even and ample heat."

"This car is wider than ours used to be, is it not?" queried Mr. Greenleaf.

"Yes," was the reply. "When the first Pullman sleeping car, the 'Pioneer,' was run on the Chicago and Alton Railroad, it was wider and higher than the ordinary coaches. Several bridges had to be raised to allow the car to pass under; and all the station platforms were altered to permit it to pass. Since then, as Pullmans and Wagners have come into use on so many roads, many changes in bridges have been found necessary, and station platforms have almost universally been cut down to the ground."

"Did I understand you to say that this is a sleeper?" asked Mr. Greenleaf. "Our sleeping cars, few and far between as they were, had berths or bunks three tiers high, fitted in on each side of the car, making it useless except to sleep in."

A PULLMAN SLEEPER.

"That was the great feature of Mr. Pullman's invention," was the reply. "He saw that few railroad companies would care to go to the expense of running cars which could only be used for sleeping purposes. He was familiar with the 'old-fashioned, stuffy cars, where men sat in stiff-backed seats and dozed and yawned and waited for morning. By putting people to sleep this wide-awake man made a fortune.' You are sitting on the bed now. But here comes the porter to make up the berths next to us. The lady wishes to put her little boy to sleep."

With much interest Mr. Greenleaf watched the porter make a sleeping room out of a sitting room. In a trice the cushions in the seats and backs were twisted about and laid from seat to seat, making a bed. With a jump, the porter stood on the arm of the seat, and turned a knob in the roof. Down came another bed, a few feet above the first. From this was pulled a triangular board which was placed between the beds and the next seats. Sheets, blankets, and pillows, which had been shut up in the roof, were soon properly spread out, and two good beds were the result. Curtains were found above the upper bed, which, hung upon poles, shut the beds off from the car aisle. Behind these the mother undressed her child and put him to bed.

Just at this moment a man went through the car crying "First call for dinner." Mr. Towne immediately jumped to his feet and said, "Let us go and get good seats."

"You have forgotten your hat, Henry," said his uncle.

"I don't need it. Come, hurry," said Henry.

Perplexed, the old man followed his nephew through three cars to the dining car, where they were soon seated at a little table, in front of a large window, from which everything they passed could be seen. It is not necessary to describe the dining room, for it was merely a well-furnished restaurant. The men ordered what they desired, and settled back to wait until their dinner was brought on.

"How is it, Henry, that we did not feel the wind as we passed from car to car? You hurried me so fast that I did not have time to notice."

"Don't you see," said the drummer, "how attaching a dining car to a train required another change also? There used to be a rule of every railroad company forbidding the passengers to go from car to car while the train was in motion. When the company put on the 'diner,' it invited the people to break its own rule. So vestibule cars came next. Side doors are built on the car platforms and with these closed the regular car doors can be left open. Thus one can walk the entire length of the train, through sleeper, parlor car, dining car, smoking saloon, library, bath room, barber shop, and writing room, without once going out of doors. This is a modern vestibule train."

One more interesting discussion took place the next morning as they were nearing New York City.

"Tell me something about modern bridges," said Mr. Greenleaf.

"Oh! I am afraid that is too long a story to tell during the time that we have left. There seems to be no limit to the engineering skill of to-day. The world-famous structures are being surpassed every little while by new ones. To-morrow you must see the Brooklyn Bridge. We have supposed that this great suspension bridge with its sixteen hundred feet from tower to tower was about the limit. But the cantilever bridge over the Forth in Scotland has a span more than a hundred feet longer than the East River bridge. When the North River bridge is built to Jersey City, with its proposed span of three thousand feet, these other great bridges will be small in comparison.

BROOKLYN BRIDGE.

"Our bridges are mostly of steel rather than wood nowadays," he continued. "Since the Portage viaduct on the Erie road, which was eight hundred feet long and two hundred and thirty feet above the river, and contained a million and a half feet of lumber, was wholly burned in 1875, wooden bridges have usually been but temporary affairs. In these days of frequent trains, the engineer's skill is needed on the shorter bridges as well as on these enormous structures. Iron towers were put in place of stone towers, and iron beams in place of wooden ones, at the Niagara Suspension Bridge, without interfering with the trains. I read the other day how a new iron bridge took the place of an old wooden one. It was built across the river by the side of the railroad track; during the night, when there was less travel than during the daytime, the old bridge was moved off, the new one took its place, and in a few minutes trains were running over it. Whatever engineering work is needed nowadays, some one will soon be found prepared to provide it."

At last the train entered the long cut and series of tunnels, which finally brought it to the Grand Central station on Forty-Second Street, New York City. Hurried along by the crowd, the aged sightseer hardly had an opportunity to make a remark about the immensity and grandeur of the brick station.

"But this station is poor and far behind the times," said Mr. Towne. "You should see some of the more modern ones that have recently been erected, or wait for the new New York station, which must soon be built. But let us hasten; I want to get home."

The young drummer, accustomed to travel of all kinds, familiar with crowds, and wont to make his way anywhere, did not realize that his companion was having difficulty in keeping up with him as he hastened along the street. Receiving no answer to a question that he asked, he glanced around to find that his uncle was not with him. Inwardly accusing himself of remissness in forgetting his companion's lack of experience, he turned and rapidly retraced his steps. He found his uncle standing on a corner, not daring to cross the street; to the relief of the latter, he decided to take a horse car across town.

Leaving the car at Sixth Avenue, the two men climbed the stairs to the elevated road. They had hardly purchased their tickets when a train drew up at the little station and a minute afterward they were off for Harlem. The horse-car ride, followed by that on the elevated road, started a discussion concerning street-car traffic. The horse car was remembered by the old missionary, who remarked that it came before the steam railroad.

Mr. Towne replied, "Yes. But its day is nearly over. New York City does not seem to have fully outgrown this slow street travel, but elsewhere more rapid transit is the rule. New York is coming to it, however. The elevated roads cannot carry all the travel—the horse cars are too slow—the size of the city demands something more than we now have."

"What do you expect will be done?" asked Mr. Greenleaf.

"We shall have to build a tunnel, an underground railway, a subway. Of course our roads must be either above ground, on the ground level, or below ground. The elevated roads have shown themselves to be unpleasant and annoying. It is not agreeable to look into the upper-story windows of dwellings, nor do people enjoy living on streets where the elevated road runs. Rapid transit is impossible in the street, where cross streets continually delay the cars, and where wagons and carriages of all sorts are regularly passing. The subway is the best method, the only decent way left open."

"Would not such a tunnel be dark and damp, dirty and unhealthy in every sense?" asked his uncle.

"Oh! no," was the reply. "Boston has recently completed a subway, something like a mile and a half long, with two branches, which has proved its great advantages. Sheltered in winter, cool in summer, never blocked by teams nor interfered with by snow or ice, brilliantly lighted, with air wholesome and dry, and less liable to accidents than any other device yet tested, the Boston Subway is a great success.

"Did you say that there was no smoke?" again asked Mr. Greenleaf.

"No smoke at all. The cars are run by electricity, and cinders are therefore entirely absent."

"Are electric cars coming into general use?" was the next question.

"Yes; throughout the country," replied Mr. Towne. "New York even now has its electric roads up town. Horse cars have been replaced by electric cars in almost every city. Cable cars are used in some places, but the electric is preferred. The last few years have seen a wonderful development in electricity in every way, but in no respect greater than in the increase of electric railways. For shorter lines they are competing with the steam cars, and seem to be winning the day. Some steam roads are equipping their lines for electric service, and report successful results so far as tried. Whether the electric car will wholly replace the steam car, time only will tell."

THE BOSTON SUBWAY.

"What a relief it must be to ride in a street car and not be obliged to pity the poor horses as they tug and strain to pull the heavy loads!" added the old missionary.

"You know, I suppose," replied the drummer, "that not only from the street cars, but in other ways the horse is being retired. The bicycle has supplanted the horse and buggy for use in thousands of families, besides being where horses could never be afforded. And now we have automobiles, or horseless carriages, run by gasoline, naphtha, or electric motors. These are expensive, and comparatively few can yet afford them for private use. They are being used to a considerable extent in large cities, especially here in New York, for public service or for the delivery of goods from our large stores. But the expenses will gradually lessen, and perhaps the day when the horse is to rest has begun."

"All this is wonderful," remarked his uncle. "We may walk still, if we wish. We may ride a horse or drive a carriage. We may take the stagecoach, or a private coach, or tally-ho. We may journey across the continent in palace steam cars. We may ride through a city on horse cars, or cable cars, or electric cars. We may travel on elevated tracks or underground. We may pedal our bicycles or ride in horseless carriages. We find good carriage roads, and excellent roadbeds for our railroads. Bridges and tunnels carry us over and under rivers, across ravines and through mountains. On the water, the canoe and the rowboat, the sailing vessel and the steamship, are at our disposal. Naphtha launches and electric yachts glide across the water. Harbors are dredged, lighthouses are erected, breakwaters are constructed, and canals are built, all for the use of travelers and commerce. The last years of the nineteenth century form an era in travel of which the world never dreamed."

ELECTRIC CAR, NEW YORK CITY.

SAMUEL F. B. MORSE.

MODERN PRINTING PRESSES.

SECTION VI.
LETTERS.

CHAPTER I.

LANGUAGE.

WHAT is the difference between a dog and a boy, or, rather, what is the difference between the brute creation and mankind? It is as natural for a dog to think as for a boy; he sees and hears and touches, smells and tastes as well as does the boy; he remembers and, in a certain way, he may be said to reason; he loves and hates and fears; he is pleased and frightened; is revengeful; has his likes and dislikes, his tastes and prejudices; indeed, a dog, or a horse, or an elephant has many points of resemblance to a boy or a man. But there are essential points of difference.

One of the most important differences is that man has the power of speech which is not possessed by the brute creation. This power of speech is a great boon to mankind, one held in common by all peoples in all ages.

Talking or conversation suggests at least two persons, the speaker and the hearer, and involves the use of the vocal organs on the part of the talker and the ear, the instrument of hearing, on the part of the listener. This power of communicating thought, as has been said, is universal with the human race.

In childhood one learns the language of his parents and of the people where he lives. In this country, Great Britain, Canada, and Australia, most of the people speak the English language; in France, the French tongue; in Russia, the Russian; in Germany, the German; in Turkey, the Arabic; and so on. This common speech forms a great bond of unity between all people of the same race, and by means of it we communicate our ideas one to another.

There is another language differing widely from the gift of speech, yet quite as important for the welfare of the human race. Barbarous and savage tribes are dependent upon speech alone, but in civilized countries the people have acquired another art, that of writing, or of using a written language. In speech arbitrary sounds represent ideas. In writing arbitrary symbols or characters, called letters and words, are used. They are observed by the eye and not by the ear. This written language is as extended, as sharp, as definite, as full and complete, as is the language of speech. Moreover, it has a great advantage over speech. Words can be spoken only to a person immediately present, but words can be written and conveyed to one who is absent. No matter how far apart two persons are, each can communicate his ideas to the other just as well as if they were near.

This written language has still greater usefulness. By means of it wise men of all countries who have had great thoughts, thoughts of value to the whole human race, have been enabled to put those thoughts into a permanent form. Thus they have been preserved and handed down from generation to generation, so that we inherit to-day the wealth of all the ages. We can make ourselves familiar with the great thoughts uttered by Jesus, by Socrates, Aristotle, Shakespeare, Milton, Burke, Patrick Henry, Daniel Webster, Emerson, Longfellow, and countless others, so that they become our own property. Moreover, when the eye gathers up these grand truths from the printed page, they are not absorbed, they still remain there. They may be used and transmitted again and again in the same book and upon the same page, even to future generations.

On one occasion King Solomon said: "Of making many books there is no end, and much study is a weariness of the flesh." The second part of this sentence is certainly very true, but that is not saying anything against study, for anything that is worth doing is a cause of weariness. When we get weary the best thing is to get thoroughly rested, and after that to work until we become weary again. It does not injure a strong, well person to get healthily tired; on the contrary, the weariness which comes from normal exercise of the hands or the brain is better than inactive ease.

ANCIENT IMPLEMENTS OF WRITING.

What did Solomon mean when he made this sage remark, "Of making many books there is no end"? Under what circumstances was the remark made? We may not be able to answer the last question literally, but we may be permitted to imagine the circumstances. Let us suppose that the Queen of Sheba had made her famous visit to Jerusalem. She had heard in her own country of the acts and the wisdom of Solomon, and had come to the kingdom of Israel to see, with her own eyes, if these reports were true. She heard his wisdom from his own lips, for he "told her all her questions."

Then the Queen of Sheba had said to Solomon: "It was a true report which I heard in mine own land of thine acts, and of thy wisdom: howbeit, I believed not their words, until I came, and mine eyes had seen it: and, behold, the one half of the greatness of thy wisdom was not told me; for thou exceedest the fame that I heard. Happy are thy men, and happy are these thy servants, which stand continually before thee, and hear thy wisdom. Blessed be the Lord thy God, which delighted in thee to set thee on his throne, to be king for the Lord thy God."

The Queen had gone home, and early one morning Solomon had risen from his couch and gone up to the flat roof of his house on Mount Zion just as the sun was rising. There in his meditations he thought to himself that the Queen of Sheba had paid him great honor and that he ought in courtesy to send her a suitable present. What should it be? He was impressed with the idea that he would send her a copy of the sacred books then in the keeping of the high priest. What present could be more appropriate, more honorable to him, more welcome to her, or more acceptable to Jehovah, the God of his people Israel?

If he sent her a copy of these books it surely ought to be a perfect copy. Books were not printed in those days; they were written with the pen, or rather with the stylus. Solomon called a servant and said to him, "Send for the chief of the scribes. Bring him here." He came, and the king directed him to select only those scribes that could do perfect work, and to set them at the task of making the finest possible copy of the books of Moses and the other sacred books.

AN ANCIENT SCRIBE.

Month after month went by, until finally the work was finished and the scribes were ushered into the royal presence, bearing in their arms the product of their long-continued labor. Roll after roll of the finest parchment was submitted to Solomon for inspection. Each skin began with an illuminated letter, and the whole work was done in the highest style of the art.

Well pleased was Solomon when these rolls were all properly packed, secured from rain, placed upon the backs of camels, and the caravan, with a military escort, had set out for the distant land of Sheba. Then again in the gray of the morning Solomon was at his meditations upon the housetop. Again he called a messenger who should summon to his presence the chief of the scribes.

"What was the cost of making the copy of our sacred writings for the Queen of Sheba? How many shekels have been paid to the scribes for their work?"

When the chief scribe had found out he reported it to the king. "Is it indeed so much?" said the king; and when he had thought how many months it had taken for that large number of scribes to make a single copy of the sacred books, then he exclaimed: "Of making *many* books there is no end."

CHAPTER II.

THE PRINTING PRESS.

The times have changed since King Solomon's day. The art of printing has been discovered. Now it would be possible to make not merely one copy but thousands of copies, not only of the sacred books of the Jews in the time of Solomon, but of the entire Bible as we have it to-day. Not in the months required by the Jewish scribes, but in a single month, thousands of copies of the whole Bible could be printed from the type set in a single establishment in Boston, New York, or Philadelphia. Surely, before the art of printing one might truly say, "Of making books there is no end." But to-day our modern press sends out its volumes by millions, so that no longer is there any truth in this apparently wise statement of Solomon. It was true in his day, but times have changed.

Two visitors were wending their way through Machinery Hall at the Centennial Exhibition in Philadelphia in 1876. Clatter, clatter, clatter—clatter, clatter, clatter—jigger, jigger, jigger—jigger, jigger, jigger. What was that great machine that they were approaching? It was the Walter press, invented in London for the London *Times*,—"The Thunderer." Well, well! the press does thunder, literally, does it not? It was printing that day's issue of the New York *Times*, and there were coming from that press about twelve thousand copies of the double-size sheet in an hour. Well might it make a racket if it accomplished such a work as that.

After the visitors were done admiring it they passed on, and a little beyond came suddenly upon another printing press which was doing its work in comparative silence. Before them stood a double Hoe perfecting press, printing the Philadelphia *Times*, turning off thirty thousand copies per hour. These came out from the machine, folded ready for the wrappers or for the newsboy to take upon his arm and run out into the street to sell! So marvelous was the work of the American press. The original invention was surprising, but the progress that has been made in making type, setting it, electrotyping and inking, and making paper, as well as in the presswork, is beyond the power of description.

There are vague, indefinite stories of printing by the Chinese a thousand years before Christ. The Greeks and Romans made metal stamps with characters engraved in relief. It was not, however, until about the middle of the fifteenth century that movable types were made with which books could be printed. The period between 1450 and 1500 witnessed a rapid advance of civilization in Europe. It was marked by a great revival of classical learning and art, and announced the dawn of modern civilization. At that time Europe began to come out into the light of reason, learning, and both civil and religious liberty. The mariner's compass had been invented; gunpowder had been discovered; and now the art of printing came into use. It would seem that no one man invented this art in the way that Stephenson invented the locomotive and Whitney the cotton gin. It grew up, one man doing a little, and another something more, until the system was brought to its present wonderful efficiency.

It has been said that Coster of Haarlem, Holland, invented wooden types about 1428 and metal types a little later. About 1440 John Faust did a little printing, and others also have claimed the invention. John Gutenberg is the only claimant who is known to have received honor during his life time as the true inventor. The evidence would seem to show that he was engaged in his secret process before the year 1440. He certainly had a printing office in 1448 at Mentz. About this time Faust came into possession of this printing office and managed it until his death. Among the earliest books printed were, "Letters of Indulgence," two editions of the Bible, and a Latin dictionary.

John Baskerville, an Englishman, devoted his life and fortune to the improvement of printing. He was born in 1706 and died in 1775. He published an edition of Vergil in royal quarto, which was then and is still considered a wonderful specimen of beautiful printing. His English Bible, Book of Common Prayer, and editions of various classics are still admired and greatly sought. A Baskerville classic is difficult to find in these days and it commands a high price; when one is found it shows great skill, judgment, and taste.

Baskerville made types much superior in distinctness and elegance to any that had previously been used. He improved greatly the lines of the letters, their style and appearance, making them as artistic as possible. To this end he planned in detail the style of all type which he used. He experimented also in the manufacture of ink to get that which had the most permanent color. He superintended the manufacture of the paper he used in order to obtain a finished surface best adapted to receive the impressions of the type.

Printing in America during the colonial days was subject to much difficulty. The first printing press in our country was set up at Cambridge in the house of the president of Harvard College, Rev. Henry Dunster, in 1639. Eliot's Bible in the Indian language was printed upon this press between 1660 and 1663. This same printing establishment is still in existence and has been known for many years as the University Press.

The first Bible printed in America in any European language was a German Bible issued in 1743 by Christopher Sower in Germantown, Pennsylvania. This was a wonderful work for those early days. It was a large quarto Bible, consisting of 1,284 pages, and it took four years to complete the printing of it.

How quaint the early printing press would appear to us of to-day! It was used with very little change for one hundred and fifty years. The "forms" of type were placed upon wood or stone beds surrounded by frames called "coffins," moved in and out by hand with great labor, and after each impression the platen which had pressed the paper down upon the type had to be screwed up again with a bar.

The presses which Benjamin Franklin used were made with wooden framework of the simplest possible construction. Iron frames were first used in England just one hundred years ago.

A FRANKLIN PRESS.

Franklin, in his Autobiography, tells the story of his attempt to set up a printing establishment in Philadelphia. At first he found it difficult to obtain any work, but finally he was given the job of printing forty sheets of a "History of the Friends." The price offered was low, but Franklin and his partner, Meredith, decided to accept it as a beginning.

Franklin set up the type for a sheet each day, while Meredith "worked it off at the press" the next day. The type had to be distributed every evening in order that it might be ready for the next day's composition. Therefore it was often late at night before Franklin finished his day's task, perhaps eleven o'clock or even later.

Other little jobs came in to delay the printers, but Franklin woas determined to do a sheet a day of the history. One night, just as his work was done, one of the forms was accidentally broken, and two pages "reduced to pi." Franklin, late as it was, distributed the pi and composed the form again before going to bed.

Such industry and perseverance were sure to bring success in the end. Though, in the clubs and markets, every one was saying that the establishment must fail, since the two other printers in town had barely enough to do, yet Dr. Baird was nearer right; he used to say: "The industry of that Franklin is superior to any I ever saw of the kind; I see him at work when I go home from the club, and he is at work again before his neighbors are out of bed."

To-day we have a great variety of printing presses which embody both science and art in skillful fashion. These range from the smallest size of hand presses, through numberless grades, varying in size, strength, power, rapidity, and ease of running, to the modern newspaper press and folder and the wonderful color printing press. One of the newspaper presses will print at one impression, from a single set of stereotype plates, papers of four, six, eight, ten, twelve, fourteen, or sixteen pages, at the rate of twelve thousand per hour, all cut at the top, pasted, and folded, with the supplement inserted at its proper place. With duplicate sets of plates, it will print sets of four, six, or eight page papers at the rate of twenty-four thousand per hour.

Let us look for a moment at the method of inking the type. Until a comparatively recent date the inking was all done by hand, by means of an inking pad. The ink is now spread over the type with almost perfect regularity by means of flexible rollers.

Great improvements have been made in typesetting. Several late inventions largely take the place of the old-fashioned setting by hand. One of these which is much used in newspaper work, and to some extent upon books and magazines, is called the linotype. By pressing the key of the proper letter upon a keyboard arranged something like a typewriter, the letter is pushed down, and when a line of letters and words has been completed, and the words properly spaced, this matrix is pressed down upon the melted type metal. The line is already stereotyped for use.

The recent processes of stereotyping and electrotyping have added greatly to the cheapness, accuracy, and beauty of printing. Nearly all books formerly printed from movable type are now either stereotyped or electrotyped, so that edition after edition may be printed from the same plates.

The art of printing has been called the "Divine Art." It is "the art preservative of all arts." To a large extent all civilization depends upon the art of printing.

CHAPTER III.

THE POSTAL SYSTEM.

WE have already seen that letters may be written and sent by mail to distant countries or cities. To send a letter to any place in our own country will cost us but two cents; to any country in Europe, but five cents. Indeed, we may send a letter to any one of the countries within the postal league,—and this includes most of the countries of Asia and South America, some parts of Africa and many islands of the sea,—for the same simple postage of five cents.

But the time was when nothing of the kind could have been done. In the "long ago" there was no post-office system in any country; no mails, regular or irregular, were sent from one place to another.

The modern postal system evidently grew out of the practice among kings of sending couriers to carry messages from one to another. In the early times some powerful rulers organized a staff of government couriers. After a time it came about that these government couriers began to carry letters from private individuals of high rank to their friends. So, in the process of time, this grew into a permanent system; that is, the government couriers were accustomed to carry private correspondence as well as the missives of the king.

This transmission of letters by special couriers sent out by the king dates back to very early times. Explorations in Egypt have brought to light specimens of these letters dating back to a period of two thousand and even three thousand years ago. Upon what do you suppose those letters, sent so long ago and preserved to the present time, were written? They could not have been written upon paper, for paper was not known in those days, and could not have been preserved through so many ages; neither were they written upon parchment or upon the skins of animals. These letters which have stood the test of time for twenty or twenty-five centuries were written upon tablets of clay or of stone.

The development of the modern postal system seems to have been begun in Great Britain. Some of the account books of the kings of England who lived about six hundred years ago have been preserved to the present time. In these are found records of letter-carrying on regular lines and at stated intervals. From this beginning the English postal system increased in efficiency and importance; when the colonists came to America they early made arrangements for the carrying of letters.

The records of the General Court of Massachusetts show that in 1639 it was enacted "that notice be given Richard Fairbanks that his house in Boston is to be the place appointed for all letters which are brought from beyond the seas or are to be sent thither to be left with him, and he is to care for them, that they are to be delivered or sent according to the directions; he is allowed for every letter a penny, and must answer all mistakes from his own neglect of this kind." In 1657 the colonial law of Virginia required "that every planter was to provide a messenger to convey the dispatches as they arrived, to the next plantation and so on, paying and forfeiting a hogshead of tobacco for default."

In 1672 it was agreed between some of the colonies along the coast that a post be sent once a month from New York to Boston. How should we be able to-day to transact business under such conditions? Now we have many mails a day between these two cities. Gradually the postal system was extended, and in 1730, Colonel Spotswood of Virginia was made Postmaster-General of the colonies by the British Government. In 1753, Dr. Franklin was made Postmaster-General. Franklin was very efficient in this office; he visited nearly all of the offices in the country in person, and introduced many improvements. In 1774, by his loyalty to the colonies, Franklin incurred the enmity of the British Government and was dismissed from the office. The next year, however, he was appointed Postmaster-General by the Continental Congress. In 1792, regular rates of letter postage were fixed by Congress, based on the distance to be sent.

The writer remembers that when he was a boy he received a letter from his mother fifteen miles away for which he had to pay six cents postage. At another time a letter was received from his sister who was a little over thirty miles away, for which he had to pay eight cents; and when a schoolmate who lived more than sixty miles distant sent him a letter, he had to pay the postmaster ten cents in order to get it. These letters were written on coarse, heavy paper with quill pens. The letter was folded, and the fold of one side was tucked into the fold of the other side so as to leave but one thickness of paper outside of that fold. The letter was sealed by a wafer or by sealing wax dropped upon the paper where the two edges came together, and stamped with a seal. On the opposite side the letter was properly addressed. There were no envelopes in those days.

See what changes have taken place within the memory of persons still living. To-day we write a letter, fold it, insert it in an envelope, and place on it a two-cent stamp; the carrier comes to the house, puts the letter in his pouch, carries it to the post office, and it is sent to California or any of the United States, Mexico or Canada, and delivered to the person to whom it is addressed.

Postage stamps were not used on mail matter by government direction until the year 1840, and it was not until 1847 that the Government issued the first stamps for general use. Prior to that, however, individual postmasters, on their own responsibility, had printed and sold postage stamps. Within a few years their use became quite general in many countries.

About the year 1850, it was noticed that stamps of different colors and design were received in the mails from various parts of the world. Then the idea of collecting stamps came into vogue. After a time children and young people generally began to collect and to study stamps. Every minute variation of paper, with style of printing, gum, water mark, and other differences was considered as making a different issue, and in some cases as many as fifty distinct styles of a single stamp have been collected.

POSTAGE STAMPS.

An extra fee of ten cents secures the immediate special delivery by messenger of any letter thus sent. Merchandise parcels can be sent as well as letters and papers. There is a money order system and at the present time a great deal of thought is put upon the question of post-office savings banks, which have already been successfully established in Great Britain and other countries of Europe.

By the Constitution of the United States, Congress has power "to establish post-offices and post-roads." Before roads were common between one State and another, the mail was carried on horseback. Later, mail wagons were used to convey the mails from one office to another. As stagecoaches multiplied they were used as mail wagons, the Government paying the stage company a sum of money for carrying the mail pouches.

The general introduction of railroads modified this system of mail carriage. Almost every railroad has become a postal road, the mail being carried upon its trains. Most of the trains upon the main lines of railroads have each a postal car fitted up with the proper conveniences for receiving and delivering the mail at the various stations and sorting it while the train is moving.

ASSORTING MAIL ON THE TRAIN.

Suppose a mail pouch to be received at New Haven; before reaching Bridgeport its contents are sorted; all that is to go to Bridgeport is put into a separate pouch and dropped off at that place; that which is to go to Greenwich is put into another pouch and left there, and so on. The mail of New York City is put into various pouches according to its destination. The mail matter for the sub-offices, like Station A and Station B, is put into separate pouches and sent from the railroad station on 42d Street directly to these offices, while that for the central office is so sorted that there is no delay in sending it out after its arrival at the office. The letters for lock boxes are placed together by sections, while those for carriers are put up in divisions so as to be delivered at once to the several carriers. Meantime mail matter which is to go beyond New York is put into proper pouches so that one can be dropped off at Trenton, another at Philadelphia, and so on.

It will readily be seen that vast improvements have been made in postal arrangements. The condition of the United States postal system has been greatly improved each year. It seems almost marvelous that the mail service is so reliable and that the transmission of mail matter is so expeditious and satisfactory. If mail matter should happen to be lost, which is very rarely the case, the facilities for finding it are sometimes quite surprising, as the following incident will show.

A young lady in Iowa sent by mail a piece of crocheted edging to her cousin in Dorchester, which is a part of Boston, Massachusetts. The contents slipped out somewhere and the wrapper was delivered to its proper address, but without the edging. A letter had already been received in which the sending of the article was mentioned, so that the receiver knew from whom the wrapper came. She notified the sub-postmaster in charge of the Dorchester office, and he began the system of tracing by means of blanks prepared for that purpose. He wrote out the description of the article and the facts of the case, and sent these blanks to the postmaster at Boston. The Boston postmaster forwarded them to Chicago; from Chicago the blanks were sent to the several offices west of Chicago until they reached the point of departure, in Iowa. No trace was found to answer the description, and the blanks came back to Chicago. They were then sent eastward. At Cleveland the missing article was found and forwarded to the postmaster at Chicago, whence the blanks had last been sent out. The Chicago postmaster forwarded the same to Boston with the missing article; from Boston the description and the merchandise were sent to Dorchester. Meantime the family had moved to Salem, and the Dorchester postmaster forwarded them to Salem. The receiver secured the missing article and receipted for the same, while the description with its various entries of travel, from Dorchester to Boston, from Boston to Chicago, from Chicago to the various offices in Iowa, then back to Chicago, thence to the different offices as far as Cleveland, and then from Cleveland to Chicago, Boston, Dorchester, and Salem, furnished a document of considerable interest.

In 1790 there were 70 post offices and 1,875 miles of post roads. That year the number of letters and papers delivered did not exceed 2,000,000. In 1890, one hundred years afterward, there were more than 65,000 post offices and more than 30,000 mail routes. During that year more than 10,000,000,000 pieces of mail matter were handled. The receipts and expenditures of the post-office department in the United States amount annually to about $75,000,000.

This résumé of the postal service plainly shows the energy, enterprise, and intelligence of our people, the success attained by our Government, and the tremendous growth and development of our country.

CHAPTER IV.

SIGNALING.

The transmission of letters from one point to another always requires time. Even when a letter is dropped into the post office it will not go until the next regular mail. It was long ago seen that occasions frequently arose when it was necessary to send messages quickly. This was especially important in times of war, when each army desired to know immediately the movements of the enemy. This necessity led to various devices for transmitting messages instantaneously. Any form of signaling would be satisfactory if the signals were visible to the eye of the distant observer.

The earliest method of signaling was the use of the beacon fire or the sending of messages by light. In the early colonial period in this country, during the anxious times of Indian hostilities, beacon poles were here and there set up and from them large kettles were suspended which held combustible matter. The burning of this material conveyed the intelligence that danger was at hand.

One of the earliest beacon poles was erected on Beacon Hill, in Boston, about 1634. A watchman was constantly at the place to give the signal on the approach of danger. That beacon pole was a tall mast, firmly supported, about seventy feet in height. Tree nails were driven into it to enable the watchman to ascend, and near its top an iron crane projected which supported an iron skeleton frame. In this frame was placed a barrel of tar to be fired when the occasion required the signal. This beacon was more than two hundred feet above the sea level, and the light of it, therefore, could be seen for a great distance inland. Many of the early settlements in New England were made upon the tops of hills in order that the people might the more quickly and easily see the approach of Indians and signal the news to other settlements by bonfires.

A second method of signaling was by the use of the semaphore. This was invented by Claude Chappe and was adopted by the French Government in 1794. It consists of an upright post, which supports a horizontal bar or arm, which can be put at various angles. In order to carry out this system of signaling, stations must previously be agreed upon and signal officers constantly on duty. If the intelligence was to be conveyed to a considerable distance intermediate stations must be had. The second station received the signal from the first and transmitted it to the third, and so on. This proved to be a very difficult operation and was never extensively used.

SIGNALING BY BEACON FIRES.

A third and successful form of signaling was by the motion of flags. During our Civil War the army made much use of military signals. The system was devised by Major Myer and was continued through the war, not only in the army but on naval vessels. When the stations were less than five miles apart signaling was considered to be at very short range. Messages have been sent ten miles by means of a pocket handkerchief attached to a twelve-foot rod. With the regular flags and staffs used by the signal corps during the war, signals were often read twenty-five miles away, and it is said that single words have been read at a distance of forty miles.

In the early spring of 1863 General Peck was in command of the Union forces at Suffolk, Virginia. He had under him about ten thousand men and had thoroughly fortified the place by a connected system of forts, redoubts, and breast-works. His outmost signal station was placed on an elevated plateau across the Nansemond River. This station was made by sawing off the top of a tall pine tree and placing thereon a small platform surrounded by a railing. The signal officer would tie his horse at the foot of the tree and mount to the platform by a rope ladder.

Early one morning in March, this signal officer suddenly observed the head of a column of troops emerging from the woods in the rear. This was the advance guard of two Confederate corps under General Longstreet. Instantly he caught up his signal flag and as quickly as possible signaled to the town the approach of the enemy. Picking up his signal book he hurried down the ladder, mounted his horse and galloped away. Before he could reach his saddle, however, the Confederates were within rifle range and fired at him. They did not succeed in hitting him and he escaped safely to his friends.

The signal had been seen and was quickly repeated to all parts of the fortified town. The drums instantly beat the long roll and, within five minutes from the time his signal was given, and before General Longstreet could swing out his light battery and open fire, the entire Federal force was under arms and the artillery in the nearest battery had opened a raking fire. The briskness of this fire from the Federal battery soon obliged Longstreet to withdraw his forces to the cover of the woods. Had it not been for the promptness of the signal officer it is possible that the town might have been captured.

A notable use of this system of army signals occurred in the campaign of General Miles against the Apaches in New Mexico and Arizona in 1886. He established a system of thirteen signal stations in that country, over which, during a period of four months, more than eighteen hundred messages were sent. The savages were surprised and confounded by the way intelligence of their movements became known hundreds of miles distant.

As early as 1861 Moses G. Farmer introduced a successful method of signaling which afterward was employed by the officers of the United States Coast Survey on Lake Superior. This system was by means of mirrors which were able to reflect the sunlight between stations ninety miles apart. This method is called the heliographic system. The French have used it among the islands of the Indian Ocean where the stations are on mountain peaks sometimes 135 miles apart. Even this long-range signaling has been surpassed by our own Signal Corps, which has succeeded in sending messages by our method from Mount Uncompahgre in Colorado to Mount Ellen in Utah, a distance of 183 miles. During the siege of Paris, messages by the use of the calcium light, concentrated and directed by lenses, were sent from one point to another.

A very unique form of signaling was employed by New York State at the opening of the Erie Canal, in 1825. The cannon, which had been captured by Commodore Perry at the time of his famous victory on Lake Erie, were placed at intervals along the line of the canal. When the first canal boat started from Buffalo, the first cannon was fired. When the sound was heard at the second cannon, that was discharged; and so on, the entire length of the canal. Two hours after the start at Buffalo the news had reached New York.

All these various methods of communication at long range have proved more or less objectionable and unsatisfactory. It was natural, therefore, that as soon as it was known that electricity could be conducted by wires from one place to another, experiments should be begun in the hope of finding some possible means of conveying intelligence by it. Perhaps the earliest suggestion was in a letter published in *The Scots Magazine*, of February, 1753. The letter was signed "C. M.", which probably meant Charles Morrison, a young Scotch surgeon. He proposed to use as many insulated conductors as there were letters in the alphabet. Each wire was to represent one letter only, and the message would be sent by charging the several wires in succession so that the operator in receiving it would be obliged to notice the order of movement among the wires. From that simple beginning inventors proceeded to suggest first one thing and then another, but they found so many difficulties that it seemed impossible to overcome them all.

CHAPTER V.
THE TELEGRAPH.

ELECTRIC WIRES.

On the second day of April, 1872, in the city of New York, the life of a benefactor of his race, an aged man who had seen more than fourscore years of mingled trial and triumph, was ended. That man was Prof. Samuel Finley Breese Morse, the inventor of the electric telegraph. His name is as widely known the world over as that of Washington, or Cæsar, or Aristotle. His long life had been extremely checkered. He had passed through troubles, trials, anxieties, disappointments, bereavements; he had been subject to persecutions, losses, poverty, toil, discouragements; he had met with successes, gains, wealth, luxury, honors, fame; and finally the homage of republics, kingdoms, empires had been laid at his feet. He was never cast down, never unduly elated. He bore all his poverty and disappointments and wore all his honors and wealth with the "grace of a Christian and the calmness of a philosopher."

Professor Morse was born at the foot of Breed's Hill in Charlestown, Massachusetts, April 27th, 1791. He was the oldest of three brothers. His father was a very distinguished man in his day; for more than thirty years the pastor of a church in Charlestown, a noted preacher, a good historian, the author of many books, and, particularly, the father of the science of geography in the United States. Professor Morse inherited from both his father and his mother those traits of character which enabled him to succeed in his great life work, in spite of discouragements, obstacles, and opposition. His ancestors were all noted for their "intelligence, energy, original thinking, perseverance, and integrity."

How we would like to step into the little schoolroom and see Samuel at his first school. He was four years of age. His teacher was known as "Old Ma'am Rand," an invalid who could not leave her chair. She governed the uneasy little urchins with a long rattan that would reach across the small room where she kept her school. At seven years of age Samuel was sent to Andover to a preparatory school, kept by Mr. Foster; here he fitted for Phillips Academy and, in that famous institution, under the direction of Mark Newman, he prepared for Yale College, where he was graduated in 1810.

While in college he was under the instruction of Jeremiah Day in natural philosophy and paid great attention to the subject of electricity, getting everything that was known about it at that time. Professor Day said: "Morse was often present in my laboratory during my preparatory arrangements and experiments, and thus was made acquainted with them." On leaving college Morse had a burning ambition to be a portrait painter. He put himself under the instruction of Washington Allston, and went with him to England to pursue his favorite study. Is it not a little singular that Morse, who invented the telegraph, was a student under Allston, and that Robert Fulton, who invented the American steamboat, was a student under West, another famous American painter?

One day Mr. Allston introduced young Morse to Benjamin West, whose fame at that time was as wide as the world of art. West was in his studio painting his "Christ Rejected." After a time he began a critical examination of Mr. Morse's hands and at length said: "Let me tie you with this cord, and take that place while I paint the hands of our Saviour." Morse of course complied; West finished his work and, releasing him, said, "You may say now, if you please, you had a hand in this picture."

Morse had many interesting experiences in England during his four years' study under Allston. He returned to America in 1815, and from that time for about fifteen years devoted himself to painting and inventing. He was for some time professor of the fine arts in the University of the City of New York, and during all these years he paid much attention to the study of electricity.

After three years spent in Europe, he returned in 1832 on the packet ship *Sully*. In the early part of the voyage, one day at the dinner table, the conversation turned to the subject of electro-magnetism. Professor Morse remarked: "If the presence of electricity can be made visible in any part of the circuit, I see no reason why intelligence may not be transmitted by electricity."

His mind could think of nothing else; this one idea had taken complete possession of his soul; all that he had learned in former years, his experiments with Professor Day at Yale College, and his later studies, were all revived and drawn upon for ways and means to accomplish the thing he had in mind. He withdrew from the table and went upon deck. He was in mid-ocean, the sky everywhere above him, the sea everywhere below him. As the lightning comes out of the east and shines unto the west, so swift and so far was that instrument to work which was taking shape in his mind.

He could not fail, for patience, perseverance, and hope were hereditary traits in his character. He was just at the maturity of manhood, forty-one years of age; from that time this one idea absorbed his mind. All his powers were concentrated upon this one subject, the electric telegraph.

Now began a series of experiences such as probably no other man ever passed through. Scarcely did any one ever suffer so much, endure so much, fail so many times to accomplish his darling object, as did Morse. He completed his invention; he perfected it. He devised his alphabet consisting of long and short marks and dots; he obtained a patent for it; but he had not the money to put the invention in operation. Years of trouble and even abject poverty followed. He was so reduced at one time that he was without food for twenty-four hours. He applied to Congress again and again for a grant to enable him to build and put in operation a trial line between Baltimore and Washington.

On the morning of the 4th of March, 1843, as Professor Morse came down to breakfast, at his hotel in Washington, a young lady met him and said:

"I have come to congratulate you, sir."

"For what, my dear friend?" asked the professor.

"On the passage of your bill."

That bill was for the appropriation by Congress of $30,000 for the purpose of "constructing a line of electric-magnetic telegraph" under the direction of Professor Morse. The bill had passed the House some days before. It had been favorably reported to the Senate, but there were a hundred and forty bills before it upon the calendar which were to be taken up in their regular order. Professor Morse had remained in the Senate chamber till late in the evening. His friends informed him that it was impossible for the bill to be reached, as the Senate was to adjourn at midnight. He had, therefore, retired to his hotel thoroughly discouraged. Imagine then, if you can, his surprise and his joy when Miss Ellsworth the daughter of his friend, Hon. H. L. Ellsworth, of Connecticut, the commissioner of patents, told him that in the closing moments of the session the bill had passed without a division.

He had invented the recording electric telegraph eleven years before on board the packet ship *Sully*, upon his return voyage from Europe. He had spent eleven years in perfecting his plans, and in striving to secure the means for placing this great invention before the American people. During this time he had converted all his property into money and used all that money in pushing the enterprise. His only hope now was the bill before Congress. That bill had passed! With streaming eyes Professor Morse thanked Miss Ellsworth for her joyous announcement, and promised her that she should dictate the first message which should be sent over the wires.

And so it came to pass that on the 24th of May, 1844, these words furnished by Miss Ellsworth were telegraphed by Professor Morse from the Capitol at Washington, to his friend and assistant, Mr. Alfred Vail, at Baltimore, and immediately repeated back again:

"What hath God wrought!"

MORSE HEARS OF HIS SUCCESS.

Well may we believe that the inventor spoke from the heart when he said years later: "No words could have been selected more expressive of the disposition of my own mind at that time, to ascribe all the honor to Him to whom it truly belongs."

A singular circumstance brought this invention to the attention of the people of the whole country as hardly anything else could have done. The National Democratic convention was in session at Baltimore. They had unanimously nominated James K. Polk for the Presidency. They then nominated Silas Wright as their candidate for Vice-President. This information was immediately telegraphed by Mr. Vail to Professor Morse and at once communicated by him to Mr. Wright, then in the Senate chamber. A few minutes later the convention was astonished by receiving a telegram from Mr. Wright, declining the nomination. The members were incredulous and declared that it was a trick of Mr. Wright's enemies. They voted to send a committee to Washington to interview Mr. Wright, and adjourned until the next morning.

On the return of this committee the truth of the message was corroborated, and thus this new telegraph, just completed, with a line just open for public pa-tronage, was advertised through the delegates of this national convention to the people of every State in the Union. Astonishment was the sensation of the hour. The work bordered upon the miraculous. Ordinarily the motto is true that "To see is to believe," but this result staggered everybody.

Although the invention was complete and now in practical operation, yet Professor Morse's trials were not over. He received the congratulations of his friends, but he was also brought to the notice of his enemies. Let us pass over these trials and give attention to the more pleasant duty of considering his triumphs. The telegraph rapidly came into general use between the great cities of the country. Nor was its use confined to America; almost immediately it was successfully introduced into the various countries of Europe.

In 1854, the Supreme Court of the United States decided unanimously in favor of Professor Morse on all points involving his right to the claim of having been the original inventor of the electro-magnetic telegraph. In 1846, Yale College conferred upon him the degree of Doctor of Laws (LL.D.). He was made a member of various learned societies in France, Belgium, and the United States. He received a diamond decoration from the Sultan of Turkey, a gold snuff box containing the Prussian gold medal for scientific merit, the great gold medal of Arts and Science from Würtemberg, and the great gold medal of Science and Art from the Emperor of Austria. Other honors were conferred upon him by Denmark, Spain, Portugal, Italy, and Great Britain. At the instance of Napoleon III., Emperor of the French, representatives from various countries met in Paris in 1858 and decided upon a collective testimonial to Professor Morse, and the result of their deliberations was a vote of 400,000 francs.

No invention in ancient or modern times has wrought such a revolution—a revolution in all business, in commerce, trade, manufacturing and the mechanic arts, in politics, government, and in religious affairs. It is not given to mortal man to comprehend the greatness, to duly appreciate the grandeur, or to measure the utility of this remarkable invention. Over the mountains, through the valleys, under the seas flies the electric current, conveying all-important items of news from place to place, from country to country, from continent to continent.

> "This electric chain from East to West
> More than mere metal, more than mammon can,
> Binds us together—kinsmen, in the best;
> Brethren as one; and looking far beyond
> The world in an electric union blest."

CHAPTER VI.

THE ATLANTIC CABLE.

THE growth of the telegraph was very much like that of the railroad. In 1844, the first line was opened, as we have seen, between Baltimore and Washington, a distance of forty miles. Within a few years lines were extended to the principal cities of the United States. In 1847, the Morse telegraph was introduced into Germany and rapidly spread over the entire continent of Europe. For the most part the wires were placed by the side of the railroad tracks,—wherever the railroad penetrated the telegraph went also.

Before many years had passed time was in a sense obliterated. Whatever happened in New York might be immediately known in Chicago. Incidents that took place in New Orleans might be narrated in Boston almost as soon as they occurred. London and Rome, Madrid and St. Petersburg, were united by the lightning rapidity of the telegraphic current. Meanwhile London and New York were as far apart as ever. News could be conveyed between the two hemispheres only by the comparatively slow-moving steamers. The next step in the development of communication must be the connecting of Europe with America by a telegraph wire.

The year before the passage of the act by which Congress provided Professor Morse with the means for completing the first telegraph line, he had stretched a wire under the water from Castle Garden, New York City, to Governor's Island in the harbor. He had thus proved that telegraph messages could be sent under water. Ten years later a "submarine telegraph" was constructed, connecting England with the continent of Europe. Other short submarine cables were laid and successfully operated. To undertake, however, to lay a cable from Europe to America, thousands of miles long and hundreds of fathoms below the surface of the ocean, was an entirely different matter. A few enthusiastic men, among them Professor Morse, believed that it could be done, but the majority of people viewed it as an impossibility.

Was there any other way to connect the two worlds by an electric wire? Might it not be possible to build a telegraph line from Europe, starting from some point in Russia, across Northern Asia, to the Behring Straits? Might not a comparatively short cable be laid to Russian America (for Alaska had not then been sold to the United States), which could connect with a telegraph line to be erected across the continent to New York City?

Think of the magnitude of this proposition! In place of laying a submarine cable across the Atlantic Ocean it was proposed to traverse the entire circuit of the earth, except the Atlantic, by a telegraph line. It was proposed to construct across the wilds of Siberia, where no railroad had been built, a telegraph line thousands of miles in length; and, besides laying a cable, to build another line of great length from the Aleutian Islands to the Pacific coast of the United States, and thence across the Rockies, where at that time there was no railroad.

The undertaking was a great one, but a company was formed for the purpose of erecting a Russian-American telegraph. Experienced men were selected from English and American telegraphers and sent to Siberia to push the work. The prospects of success for the great enterprise were favorable when the news arrived that the long-talked-of Atlantic cable was at last laid and in complete working order. The Russian-American telegraph could not hope to compete with the cable, and the project was abandoned.

To Cyrus W. Field belongs the honor of pushing forward to successful completion the Atlantic cable. At the early age of fifteen Cyrus left the parsonage at Stockbridge, Connecticut, the home of his father, Rev. David Dudley Field, for New York. On arriving in the city he obtained employment as an errand boy in the dry-goods establishment of A. T. Stewart. Three years later, when he decided to give up his place as clerk in the store, the proprietor showed his appreciation of the boy's merits by urging him to remain, making him a liberal offer if he would do so. He decided to make a change, however, and was soon engaged with a brother in Lee, Massachusetts.

When young Field was twenty years of age he went into business for himself, and for the next thirteen years was known as one of New York's successful merchants. He then retired from active business, but found it a difficult task to do nothing. After a long voyage to South America, he returned to New York, where he gladly welcomed the opportunity that then came to busy himself.

The Newfoundland Electric Telegraph Company had been engaged for a year in the work of erecting a line on that island, preparatory to connecting it with the mainland by a cable. The company was compelled to stop work, however, for lack of the necessary means to continue. The leading member of the company, Frederick N. Gisborne, appealed to Mr. Field for material assistance. After several interviews, in the course of which he became deeply interested in the scheme, Mr. Field came to the conclusion not only that the plan of connecting Newfoundland with the United States was feasible, but also that Newfoundland was the best starting point for a cable to Ireland.

With characteristic energy Mr. Field went at once to work. He formed a new company and obtained extensive privileges from the governments of Newfoundland, Prince Edwards Island, and the State of Maine. Many months were spent in erecting the land telegraph across Newfoundland, over wild marsh and waste moor, rocks, hills, and forests. A cable, obtained in England, was unsuccessfully laid across the Gulf of St. Lawrence in 1855. The next year a second attempt was successful. The preliminary work was now completed.

More means and more influence were needed. Mr. Field organized in London the Atlantic Telegraph Company, and showed his own faith by personally subscribing for one-quarter of the stock. The governments of Great Britain and the United States liberally aided the new company and furnished ships for laying down the cable.

On the 7th of August, 1857, the *Niagara* and the *Agamemnon* sailed from Ireland, each carrying 1,250 miles of cable. The *Niagara* began paying out her line and all went well for three days. At nine o'clock on the evening of the tenth, however, the cable ceased working. Three hours later the electric current returned, to the intense relief of all; but before morning came the cry, "Stop her! back her! the cable has parted!"

With flags at half-mast the ships returned to Ireland. Half a million dollars had been lost already. Disheartened, but not discouraged, the company voted to increase its capital and try again the next year. This time the two steamers sailed directly to mid-ocean, spliced the two parts of the cable, and sailed away from each other, the *Agamemnon* for Ireland and the *Niagara* for Newfoundland. On the 17th of August the extremities of the cable were connected with the instruments and the work was done. In the space of thirty-five minutes there was flashed under the ocean the message:

"Europe and America are united by telegraph. Glory to God in the highest; on earth peace; good will toward men."

LAYING AN OCEAN CABLE.

Messages and replies from the Queen to the President of the United States and from the mayor of London to the mayor of New York followed. The American people were wild with enthusiasm; they declared the Atlantic cable to be the greatest achievement of the age, and they heaped boundless praise upon the head of the persistent and courageous Field. Eighteen days afterward, the signals became unintelligible and the first Atlantic cable ceased to work.

Was all the time and money so far spent thrown away? No! for this first experiment paved the way for another and successful attempt. It is said also that one message, sent during these few days, saved the commercial world no less a sum than two hundred and fifty thousand dollars. For the time being, however, the project of an Atlantic cable was allowed to remain quiet.

THE GREAT EASTERN.

Mr. Field was financially ruined. The Civil War in the United States occupied the thoughts of all for several years. But in time the company was ready to try again. A newly prepared cable was made, the twenty-three hundred miles of which weighed more than four thousand tons. The largest vessel in the world, the *Great Eastern*, was employed to carry and lay it. On July 23d, 1865, the steamer started from Ireland and continued on its westward course until August 2d; then the cable parted, more than a thousand miles from the starting point. Nine days were spent in attempts to grapple for the cable, but all in vain.

The next year the *Great Eastern* again set sail, with a new cable and with sufficient wire to complete the cable of the previous year, if possible. In fourteen days the steamer entered the harbor in Newfoundland. Two months later the same steamer again reached Newfoundland, having captured the missing end of the other wire, thereby completing two cables from Europe to America.

July 27th, 1866, was a joyous day in the life of Cyrus W. Field. For thirteen years he had thought of little else but the submarine cable. Failure after failure had not discouraged him; loss of property only stimulated him to further efforts. Now success had come. The new cable was more substantial than the other of eight years before. That had failed, but this would succeed. It did succeed. From that day to this telegraphic communication between Europe and America has been constant.

Submarine cables are now in extensive operation in all parts of the world. More than half a dozen cross the Atlantic, and lines have been constructed from England to India, from India to Australia, and from the United States to Mexico and South America. At the present time there are perhaps two hundred cables belonging to companies, and about five hundred belonging to government systems. These cables, all told, cover a distance of nearly a hundred thousand miles.

A recent incident is told that shows something of the greatness of the telegraph. In June, 1897, a great celebration took place in London, in honor of the sixty years that Queen Victoria had been upon the British throne. The Queen rode in a procession through streets packed with millions of people. Just as she left the palace she pressed an electric button. Instantly this message was sent to her colonies all over the world:

"From my heart I thank my beloved people. May God bless them. Victoria, R. I."

To forty different points in her empire sped the electric message. In sixteen minutes a reply came from Ottawa in Canada; then one by one answers came in from more remote provinces; until, before the Queen reached London Bridge, the Cape of Good Hope, the Gold Coast of Africa, and the great continent of Australia had sent responses to her message.

CHAPTER VII.
THE TELEPHONE.

When the telegraph was invented, years ago, it seemed little less than a miracle that a message could be dictated in one city and received almost instantaneously in another city far distant from the sender. Scientists, however, began at once on the invention of something more wonderful. The telegraph lacks in one respect. By it messages must be sent exactly as dictated and cannot be corrected until the reply is received. In a sense, sending and receiving messages by telegraph is a form of conversation, but a conversation at arm's-length. To carry on a real conversation at long distances would be a great advance. An instrument prepared for this purpose would be called a telephone.

In 1875 Alexander Graham Bell invented the first successful electric telephone. This was exhibited at Salem, Massachusetts, and at Philadelphia at the Centennial Exhibition, and a patent for it was obtained. The apparatus of Bell's telephone is very simple, and practically consists of four parts: the battery, the wire which runs from the speaker to the hearer, a diaphragm against which the vibrations of the air produced by the voice of the speaker strike, and another diaphragm at the other end of the wire which reproduces similar vibrations and sends them to the ear of the listener. Elisha Gray of Boston made a similar invention and applied for a patent two hours after Bell's application was filed. The invention of Mr. Bell has proved a decided success. All telephonic operations, since this invention, have been based upon the instrument which he patented in 1876.

Mr. Bell was the son of a distinguished Scotch educator, Alexander Melville Bell. The father is noted for the invention of a new method for improving impediments in speech. This system of instruction is called "Bell's Visible Speech." It is used with great success in teaching deaf-mutes to speak.

His son Alexander was born in Edinburgh in 1847 and was educated at the University of Edinburgh. He removed to London when he was twenty years of age and was for a time in the University there. Three years later he went to Canada with his father, and at the age of twenty-five took up his residence in the United States, and became professor of vocal physiology in Boston University. He had been in this country but three years when he made his great invention, and its complete success gave him immense wealth. Later he invented the "photophone," in which a vibratory beam of light is substituted for a wire in conveying speech. This instrument has attracted much attention but has not proved of practical use. Professor Bell is a member of various learned societies and has published many scientific papers. His present home is in Washington.

A TELEPHONE.

Within ten years the art of telephoning has rapidly developed. This has stimulated inventions and brought into use a vast number of special contrivances for local and long-distance transmission. The principal inventors of these new contrivances are Bell, Berliner, Edison, Hughes, Dolbear, Gray, Blake, and Peirce.

Nearly all of the telephone business of our country is carried on under licenses from the American Bell Telephone Company. The telephone lines at present in the United States would aggregate a distance of more than six hundred thousand miles, and there are more than half a million instruments in our country alone. The longest telephone line extends from Portland, Maine, via Boston, New York, and Chicago, to Milwaukee, a distance of more than thirteen hundred miles.

Let us consider for a moment the wonders of this marvelous invention, as compared with another no less marvelous in its way.

In 1867 Anson Burlingame was appointed by the Chinese Government special envoy to the United States and the great European governments, with power to frame treaties of friendship with those nations. This was an honor never before conferred on a foreigner. Mr. Burlingame accepted the appointment and, at the head of a large mission of distinguished Chinese officials, arrived in this country early in 1868, negotiated with our Government the "Burlingame Treaty," proceeded the same year to England, thence to France, the next year to Denmark, Sweden, Holland, and Prussia, and finally reached Russia early in 1870. He died in St. Petersburg after a few days' illness, on the 23d of February.

ALEXANDER BELL USING A LONG-DISTANCE TELEPHONE.

Now see what the telegraph did. His death occurred about half-past nine in the morning. As soon as possible the fact was telegraphed to our minister in Paris. He forwarded the news to our minister in London; by him it was cabled across the Atlantic, transmitted from the cable to Washington and delivered to Nathaniel P. Banks, a member of the House of Representatives from Massachusetts. General Banks read the dispatch to the House, and delivered offhand an extended eulogy upon the distinguished son of Massachusetts. That speech of General Banks was written out, sent to the telegraph office, transmitted by the electric current to the various cities of the country, put into type, printed in the evening newspapers, and the writer of this chapter read it at four o'clock in the afternoon of the same day that Mr. Burlingame died. This was done as early as 1870.

But what is that compared to the greater wonders of the telephone? That a man can "talk into" the little instrument, and his voice be heard and recognized, and his words understood, by his friend in a city five hundred or one thousand miles away, is indeed a miracle. Consider for a moment what is done by means of the switchboard in the central telephone office of a great city. Every one of the thousands of subscribers has his own instrument for transmitting and receiving messages. One of these subscribers rings a bell in his house or his business office which rings another bell at the central station; the attendant inquires "Hello! what number?" and receives a reply, "four, naught, eight, Tremont." The attendant by a simple switch, turned by a touch of the hand, makes the connection and rings the bell of that subscriber whose number is "408 Tremont." Number "408 Tremont" steps to the instrument and in a quiet voice says "Hello! who is it?" Thus these two persons are placed in direct communication, and can talk with each other, back and forth, as long as they please.

This conversation is carried on between two different sections of the city where these two men live, but the same conversation may with equal ease be carried on between Boston and New York, between Boston and Washington, or between New York and Chicago. Thus time and distance are annihilated and the whole world stands, as it were, face to face.

But the marvel does not end here. The above conversation is carried on by means of a continuous wire which runs from one place to the other. If there are parallel wires, strange to say, the vibrations carried on in the one wire are liable to create, by induction, similar vibrations in the parallel wire. Here is an illustration:

Nearly twenty years ago, soon after the invention came into use, three gentlemen in Providence, Rhode Island, put up a private line between their three houses, making a circuit. Upon this line they carried on experiments and made a number of important discoveries. The evening was the time when they principally used their private telephone line. On a certain Tuesday evening these three gentlemen, conversing one with another, suddenly found themselves listening to strains of music. All three of them heard the same thing: the sound of a cornet and of one or two other musical instruments; then singing and a soprano voice. They wrote down the names of the pieces that were sung and the tunes that were played upon the instruments. They had no knowledge of the source of these sounds.

The next day, and for days following, these gentlemen went about the city inquiring of their friends everywhere if they knew of a concert on that Tuesday night where such pieces were sung and such tunes were played. Nobody had any knowledge of the affair. At length one of the gentlemen published an article in the Providence *Journal*, describing what he had heard through his telephone wire on that Tuesday evening, giving the date, and asking any one who could inform him what the concert was and where it was, to give him the desired information. Then it transpired that this concert was a telephonic experiment.

The performers were at Saratoga, New York, and they were connected by a telephone wire with friends in New York City. The experiment had plainly demonstrated that the sounds made in singing and in playing numerous instruments could be clearly understood, by means of the telephone, from Saratoga to New York City. But it proved more than this. The vibrations in that telephone wire between Saratoga and New York induced the same vibrations in the parallel wire of the Western Union Telegraph Company. These vibrations were continued through New York City to Providence and onward. The private telephone line of these gentlemen was parallel to the wire of the Western Union Company which had been thus affected, and these vibrations were picked off from the telegraph wire and conveyed by this parallel telephone wire to the receivers at these three houses.

What will be the next wonderful invention? The telegraph transmits your thoughts and delivers them in writing; the telephone transmits your thoughts and delivers them to the ear by sounds. Some day, perhaps, you may step into a cabinet in Boston and have your photograph taken in New York City by aid of an electric wire, the telephote. Just as the telephone transmits the sounds, the telephote may transmit the light and give not only light and shade, but the colors of the solar spectrum.

CHAPTER VIII.

CONCLUSION.

We have now considered six groups of topics connected with the growth and development of our country. We have looked into the houses of the Indians and of the settlers in the colonial times, and into the larger and more elaborate homes of to-day. We have considered improved means of heating and better methods of lighting. We have noticed improvements in machinery for planting, cultivating, and harvesting the products of the soil. We have seen the great advance that has been made in the manufacture of our clothing, through improved cotton and woolen machinery and the sewing machine. We have traveled by land and by water, at home and abroad, on foot, on horseback, in stagecoaches, by canals, steamboats, and railroads. Finally we have read and thought and studied about language, the printing press, our postal system, the telegraph and the telephone.

We have seen our country when it was wholly east of the Mississippi River, whereas now it is extended even to the great western ocean. A century ago our territory embraced about eight hundred thousand square miles; now it is nearly five times as great, with large areas of recently acquired Spanish islands to be added to that. The population of the United States in 1790 was less than four millions; a hundred years later it was sixty-three millions. It is now probably between seventy and seventy-five millions. Our exports then were about fifty million dollars in value; this year they are more than one thousand millions. A century since, we imported into this country goods to the value of about seventy million dollars. This was largely in excess of our exports. To-day our exports are of far greater value than our imports.

At the beginning of our national government we were almost altogether engaged in the pursuits of agriculture. Now our people are largely massed in cities and large towns, while our mechanical and manufacturing interests are of immense proportions.

A hundred years ago the people speaking the seven principal languages of Europe numbered about one hundred and fifty millions. To-day they number about four hundred millions. The present number is therefore almost three times that of a century ago. At that time the English-speaking people ranked fifth among the seven, and numbered but twenty millions. To-day they lead the list, and number one hundred and twenty millions; there are six times as many people to-day using the English language as there were a century ago. The inhabitants of our country outnumber all other English-speaking people in the whole world.

Our country occupies, all things considered, the best portion of the world. This includes the Atlantic slope, the great Mississippi basin, and the Pacific slope, and our whole territory, except our new colonial possessions, lies within the north temperate zone. We therefore have a great variety of soil and climate; the soil is the most fertile and the climate the most salubrious of the whole earth. We have an almost infinite variety of productions and our people are engaged in the entire round of human industries.

The United States has made vast strides in industry, in wealth, in intelligence, and in the comforts of life. Civilization has rapidly advanced during the whole of this century. If the great contest of the future is to be between the Anglo-Saxon race and the rest of the world, surely this great republic must have the leading position in that contest.

The American people to-day form a nation of readers. In newspapers, magazines, and books of all sorts and upon every subject the American press is prolific. We have a system of public schools well established in every State and every Territory of our Union, and supported by taxation, and very generally the children are obliged by compulsory laws to attend school. We are living in an age of great activity and rapid advancement. The young people of our republic who are attending school to-day are to be congratulated upon their good fortune; and it becomes them to magnify their opportunities, to appreciate their advantages, and to be especially loyal to their country, its government, and its institutions.

INDEX.

Lector House believes that a society develops through a two-fold approach of continuous learning and adaptation, which is derived from the study of classic literary works spread across the historic timeline of literature records. Therefore, we aim at reviving, repairing and redeveloping all those inaccessible or damaged but historically as well as culturally important literature across subjects so that the future generations may have an opportunity to study and learn from past works to embark upon a journey of creating a better future.

This book is a result of an effort made by Lector House towards making a contribution to the preservation and repair of original ancient works which might hold historical significance to the approach of continuous learning across subjects.

HAPPY READING & LEARNING!

LECTOR HOUSE LLP
E-MAIL: lectorpublishing@gmail.com